Linda's *winter* Kitchen

Linda's *winter* Kitchen

LINDA McCARTNEY

FOOD CONSULTANT
Rosamond Richardson

PHOTOGRAPHY
Debbie Patterson

TED SMART

To my family and all veggies,
present and future

A Little, Brown Book

This edition produced for The Book People Ltd,
Hall Wood Avenue, Haydock, St Helens WA11 9UL
by Little, Brown and Company

The recipes were originally published in Great Britain in 1995
by Little, Brown and Company in *Linda's Kitchen*
Introduction copyright © 1995 and 1997 by MPL Communications Ltd
Text and Photographs copyright © 1995 and 1997 by
Little, Brown and Company (Inc.)

ISBN 0-316-63976-1

A CIP catalogue for this book is available from the British Library

Food styling by Jane Suthering
Design by Janet James
Typeset by Peter Coombs
Leaves illustration by Nadine Wickenden
Printed and bound in Italy by Lego Spa

Little, Brown and Company (UK)
Brettenham House, Lancaster Place, London WC2E 7EN

The author would like to thank Paul, Heather, Mary, Stella, James, Louise, Robby
and team, Viv and team, Carol Judy and team, Geoff, Pat, Sherrie, Marie,
Sue, Shelagh, Louise, Laura, Monique, Ann, Mike, Ian, Tim and team, John, Sharon,
Maxine and everyone who helped and shared a veggie recipe.

Contents

Introduction

When my husband asked me why I was writing another cookbook, it made me realize how time had flown – and how far vegetarian cuisine had progressed in the intervening years. When I wrote my first cookbook, it was to show my family and friends how easy it was to become a vegetarian. But now our eating habits have changed, most of us are trying to cut down on fatty foods, and I felt the time had come to bring things up to date and to increase the range of easily prepared recipes that are available to today's cook.

Even if you find cooking daunting, I hope to bring out the creative cook in you. It may be that you've always thought of vegetarian meals as tiresome to prepare and bland in taste – in which case there's a surprise in store for you. Vegetarian cooking is easy, it's tasty, and it's good for your body too. Recent research has shown that a vegetarian diet can dramatically lessen the risk of – amongst other things – heart disease, angina, cancer, diabetes and high blood pressure.

Some people believe that they are vegetarian if they just cut out red meat, but a vegetarian eats no meat, and no fish either. If you go veggie, it means no animal dies for your plate. I've met a lot of people who say, "I'm almost veggie, but I still eat fish." To me that's like being "almost pregnant" – either you are or you aren't. I know that for some people cutting out fish is the most difficult obstacle on the road to vegetarianism. But fish have feelings too, and anyone who has ever seen a fish hooked out of the water, jerking and gasping for breath, should realize that. The "bountiful sea" does *not* exist for us to plunder at will, and perhaps if we started thinking in terms of sea*life* instead of sea*food* our appetite for fish might be lost.

Of course tradition is responsible for much of today's meaty diet. For most of us in the West, meat and two veg is a standard meal and, for many people, Sundays are not complete without a roast meat dinner. But the world has changed since those traditions developed. Many more people

share this planet and, as the population grows, it is simply not going to be possible to feed everyone on a meat-based diet. There just isn't enough grazing land for all the livestock required.

For me, that's a good enough reason in itself for becoming a vegetarian – because if we fed the starving people of the world the grain we use to fatten farm animals there really could be enough to go round. If everyone in the West reduced their meat consumption by just ten per cent, it would free up enough grazing land to grow food for up to 40 million people. So, being a vegetarian is not only better for you, it's better for everyone.

There are other lives that will be saved if you go veggie – the lives of the millions of animals that are slaughtered every year.

Butchered in such horrific ways that if slaughterhouses had glass walls, we'd all be vegetarian. So, be a life-saver and a world-saver, and start a whole new way of life.

There are meals for all to enjoy here – from vegan meals to meals for the truck driver who reckons he'd miss his meat (...but he won't), to kids' meals, low-calorie meals, meals for entertaining and family meals. While you're cooking, don't be afraid to adapt these recipes to suit yourself. I've tried to make taste the main ingredient in all of them; so get into the kitchen, rattle those pots and pans, have fun, and save lives while you're doing it – yours, the animals' and the planet's.

Linda McCartney

WINTER MENU PLANNER

A LUNCH FOR 4

Lentil soup 12

Stuffed
baked potatoes 63

Caesar salad 78

Lemon drizzle cake 100

AN INDIAN MENU
FOR 6

Mushroom
triangles (x1½) 28

Simple vegetable
curry (x2) 44

Easy cauliflower
dhal 44

Curried pasta salad
(x1½) 78

Curried chick peas
with onions (x1½) 45

Simple saffron rice
(x1½) 57

TWO FAMILY
SUPPERS FOR 3-4

Meatless meatballs 38
with spaghetti
and rich tomato sauce 86

Green salad with garlic
mustard dressing 82

Bakewell tart 95

Beanburgers 46

Rich tomato sauce 86

Stuffed
baked potatoes 63

Steamed vegetables

Cobbler made with
apples 90

A Christmas
Dinner for 10

Vegetable soup (x1½) 13

Cottage crunch
casserole (x1½) 40

Gravy 88

Cheese and parsley
sauce (x2) 85

Sauté of
sweet potatoes (x3) 62

Steamed vegetables

Pasta shells
with leeks (x2) 50

Vegetable
purée (x1½) 29

Lemon soufflé tart 96

Chocolate mousse 97

A Thanksgiving
Dinner for 10

Potato and carrot
soup (x1½) 16

Meatless loaf 36
with Yorkshire puddings 32
and gravy 88

Creamy potato and
leek bake 61

Aubergine and herb
casserole (x2) 41

selection of salads

Plum cobbler 90

Chocolate mousse 97

A Dinner Party for 6

Party eggs 24

Winter lasagne 53

Green salad with
poppy seed dressing 82

Lemon soufflé tart 96

Sunday Lunch
for 6 non-veggies

Aubergine caviar (x2) 24

Toad-in-the-hole 33

Spinach purée 29

Potato and cabbage
mash (x2) 62

Gravy 88

Apple sponge pudding 93

A Halloween
Supper for 10

Party eggs (x2) 24

Parsnip and
butter bean soup (x2) 18

Baked sweetcorn
pudding (x2) 32

Macaroni special (x2) 52

Curried chick peas
with onions (x2) 45

Greek rice (x2) 56

selection of salads

Apple pie (x2) 92

SOUPS

ONE OF THE JOYS OF COOKING WITHOUT MEAT IS MAKING SOUPS, USING THE ABUNDANT HARVEST OF FRESH INGREDIENTS (EVEN IN WINTER) WITH THEIR VARIED COLOURS, FLAVOURS AND TEXTURES. SPICES ENHANCE THE FLAVOURS, AND FRESH HERBS ADD QUALITIES ALL THEIR OWN. SOUPS ARE HIGHLY NUTRITIOUS AS WELL, FULL OF VEGETABLE PROTEIN, AND RICH IN VITAMINS AND MINERALS.

RUSSIAN BORSCHT v

FOR 6

6 large beetroot, peeled

1 potato, peeled

8oz (250g) green cabbage

1 large onion, chopped finely

2 tbs olive oil

4oz (125g) tomatoes, skinned (see page 13) and chopped

4 pints (2.25 litres) vegetable stock

2 tbs fresh lemon juice

sea salt and freshly ground black pepper

1/4 pint (150ml) soured cream (optional)

chopped fresh dill to garnish

This famous soup from Russia is hearty and satisfying, a warming soup for winter weather. You can make a meal of it with some warm granary bread.

METHOD: Slice the beetroot, potato and cabbage very finely, then cut the slices into matchsticks. Brown the onion lightly in the oil for 3–4 minutes, then add the rest of the vegetables and stir together for several minutes. Pour in enough stock to cover and bring to the boil. Simmer for 20–30 minutes or until tender.

Add the rest of the stock and the lemon juice. Purée half of the soup in a blender or food processor, then return it to the remaining soup in the pan and reheat gently. Season to taste. Put a dollop of soured cream on each bowl of soup (vegans can omit this) and garnish with chopped dill.

LENTIL SOUP v

FOR 6–8

1¼ lb (550g) green lentils, soaked for 2-3 hours

3½ pints (2 litres) water

2 tsp sea salt

2 tbs olive oil

1 large onion, chopped

2 stalks celery, chopped

3 carrots, sliced

2 cloves garlic, crushed

2 x 14oz (400g) cans chopped tomatoes with juice

2 tbs red wine (optional)

2 tbs fresh lemon juice

2 tbs brown sugar

2 tbs wine vinegar

freshly ground black pepper

chopped fresh thyme, oregano or basil, or chopped fresh tomatoes, to garnish

This is a real country soup, thick and warming. Adding three or four fried, sliced vegetarian sausages to this soup just before serving will turn it into a hearty main dish.

METHOD: Put the lentils in a large pan and add the water. Bring to the boil, then cover and simmer for 20 minutes. Add the salt.

Meanwhile, heat the oil in another pan and cook the onion, celery, carrot and garlic gently, covered, for about 10 minutes or until soft.

Add the softened vegetables to the lentils and stir to mix. Add the tomatoes, wine, lemon juice, sugar and wine vinegar. Season with pepper. Bring to the boil, then leave to simmer gently, uncovered, for about 30 minutes or until the lentils are very tender. If the soup becomes too thick, add a little more water.

Check the seasoning and stir in chopped fresh herbs or tomatoes before serving.

VEGETABLE SOUP v

FOR 6-8

2 tbs olive oil

1 large onion, chopped

3 leeks, sliced thinly

1 clove garlic, crushed

1 head celery, chopped

4 large carrots, sliced

½ small white cabbage, shredded

12 oz (350 g) new potatoes, cubed

1 tsp each chopped fresh thyme and rosemary

4 pints (2.25 litres) vegetable stock

8 medium tomatoes, skinned (see right) and chopped, or 1 x 14 oz (400 g) can chopped tomatoes with their juice

1 tbs chopped fresh tarragon (optional)

sea salt and freshly ground black pepper

I made this soup when invited by Pierre Franey of the New York Times to be his guest on his 'Great Cooks' series. It is warming winter food.

METHOD: Heat the oil in a heavy saucepan and lightly brown the onion, leeks, garlic and celery for 5 minutes. Add the carrots, cabbage and potatoes and stir well. Stir in the thyme and rosemary. Cover with the stock and bring to the boil. Cover and leave to simmer until the vegetables are tender, stirring and testing occasionally.

Add the tomatoes and tarragon (if using) and stir them in. Season to taste and heat through. Serve with warm wholemeal rolls.

SKINNING PEPPERS

Cut peppers into quarters and deseed. Cut each quarter into two or three strips and place skin-side up under a hot grill. Grill for 5–6 minutes or until the skin has blistered and blackened. Remove, place in a brown paper bag and cool. The skin will peel off easily.

SKINNING TOMATOES

Put tomatoes into a large bowl and cover with boiling water. Leave to stand for about 5 minutes. Lift out one by one and pierce the skin with a sharp knife; the skin will peel off easily.

TUSCAN BEAN AND CABBAGE SOUP ♥

FOR 6

2 tbs olive oil

1 large onion, sliced

2 medium carrots, sliced thin

2 medium turnips, sliced thin

2-3 cloves garlic, crushed

12oz (350g) cabbage, shredded

2 tbs chopped parsley

2 x 14oz (400g) cans cannellini or butter beans, drained (or equivalent cooked dried, see page 106)

4 tomatoes, skinned (see page 13) and chopped, or 4 canned tomatoes

3½ pints (2 litres) vegetable stock

2 tbs finely chopped parsley to garnish

sea salt and freshly ground black pepper

finely grated cheese to hand around (optional)

This soup is nourishing and satisfying, and is delicious at any time of year, especially in cold weather. Serve with Italian bread such as ciabatta.

METHOD: Heat the oil in a large saucepan and cook the onion gently for 5 minutes, covered. Then add the carrots and turnips and stir until coated with oil. Stir in the garlic. Cook gently for 2–3 minutes.

Stir in the remaining ingredients and bring to the boil. Cover and simmer gently for 25 minutes or until the vegetables are tender. Season to taste, and add more stock if necessary. Serve sprinkled with chopped parsley, and provide a bowl of finely grated cheese to pass around for those who want it.

DUMPLINGS ♥

Dumplings are a mainstay of the family cook, and can be served with any of your favourite meatless meals. For 8 dumplings mix 4oz (125g) plain or wholemeal flour (or 2oz of each combined if preferred) with 2oz (50g) vegetable suet and season well with sea salt and freshly ground black pepper. Add enough cold water to mix to an elastic dough. Shape into 8 dumplings and cook in simmering stock for 20–25 minutes. You can add a tablespoon of grated cheese (such as Parmesan) and some fresh basil, chives or parsley to the basic dough as a variation.

POTATO AND CARROT SOUP ᵥ

FOR 6

2 tbs olive oil

1 large onion, chopped

2 large potatoes, peeled and diced

8 large carrots, diced

3 pints (1.75 litres) vegetable stock, or water and 3 vegetable stock cubes

skimmed or soya milk to thin out

sea salt and freshly ground black pepper

chopped parsley to garnish

A warming, comforting soup for cold weather. Make it more substantial by adding a few crisp vegetarian steak chunks.

METHOD: Heat the oil in a large pan and cook the onion gently, covered, until soft. Add the potatoes and carrots and stir well. Pour in the stock, bring to the boil and leave to cook over a low heat, partly covered, for 30–40 minutes or until all the vegetables are very soft and tender.

Purée three-quarters of the soup in a blender or food processor. Mix with the remainder of the soup and reheat briefly, thinning out with milk if required. Season to taste and serve hot, sprinkled with parsley.

GREEN SOUP WITH PARSLEY ᵥ

FOR 4

6oz (175g) dried split peas

2 tbs olive oil

1 medium onion, chopped

4 stalks celery, sliced

2 carrots, sliced

3 tbs chopped parsley

1 bay leaf

1½ pints (900ml) vegetable stock

sea salt and freshly ground black pepper

chopped parsley to garnish

The celery flavour in this soup is highlighted by the subtle taste of split peas. It is a deliciously wholesome soup, perfect for cold weather.

METHOD: Cover the split peas with hot water and leave to soak for 1 hour. Drain and set to one side.

Heat the oil in a large saucepan and sauté the onion for 3–4 minutes. Add the celery and carrots and cook over moderate heat until lightly browned. Add the drained split peas, the parsley and bay leaf. Pour in the stock and stir well. Cover the pan and bring to the boil, then leave to simmer for 1–1½ hours or until the split peas are very tender. Add more water or stock if needed.

Season to taste and serve immediately, sprinkled with chopped parsley.

THICK ARTICHOKE SOUP

FOR 4

2 lb (1 kg) Jerusalem artichokes, peeled

2 pints (1.2 litres) vegetable stock

½ onion, finely chopped

1 tbs olive oil

5 tbs crème fraîche or single cream

sea salt and freshly ground black pepper

This simple soup has the most amazing flavour, and is a meal in itself with wholemeal rolls.

METHOD: Put the artichokes in a saucepan, cover with cold water and bring to the boil. Cover and simmer until completely soft. Cool in the liquid, then drain.

Turn the artichokes into a blender or food processor, add half of the vegetable stock and blend until smooth, then gradually add the rest of the stock. Alternatively, press the artichokes through a sieve and stir in the stock.

Cook the onion in the oil until translucent. Meanwhile, reheat the soup.

Stir the onion and crème fraîche or single cream into the hot soup and season to taste.

VEGETABLE STOCK v

MAKES – as much as you like!

vegetable scraps, such as onion, carrot, leek, cabbage, tomato, broccoli, cauliflower, Jerusalem artichoke, potato peelings

cold water to cover

sea salt

black peppercorns

bay leaves

fresh herbs in season or dried herbs

This is the basis of many soups. It is worth getting into the habit of making vegetable stock regularly, so that you always have some when you need it.

METHOD: Put the vegetable scraps or trimmings into a large saucepan and cover with cold water. Add a little sea salt, a sprinkling of black peppercorns and a couple of bay leaves for flavour. Add a small bunch of fresh herbs – such as sage, parsley, thyme, chives and/or tarragon – according to season, or a tablespoon or so of dried mixed herbs.

Bring to the boil and simmer, covered, for 45 minutes. Then leave to stand until cold.

Strain, and store in the refrigerator for up to 5 days.

PARSNIP AND BUTTER BEAN SOUP

FOR 4

2 tbs olive oil

1 large onion, chopped

3 large cloves garlic, sliced

2 large parsnips, washed and chopped

3 medium potatoes, washed and chopped

1 x 14oz (400g) can butter beans (or equivalent cooked dried, see page 106)

1½ pints (900ml) vegetable stock

1 bay leaf

1 tbs fresh lemon juice

4 tbs crème fraîche or single cream

1 pint (600ml) soya milk or skimmed milk

sea salt and freshly ground black pepper

Wonderful winter food, this soup is highly nutritious, very warming and full of flavour. Sweet parsnips make particularly delicious soups that are economical too.

METHOD: Heat the oil in a heavy saucepan and stir in the onion and garlic. Cover and cook gently for 8–10 minutes or until softened. Add the chopped parsnips and potatoes and stir well, then add the butter beans with the juices from the can. Pour in the vegetable stock and add the bay leaf and lemon juice. Bring to the boil, then cover and leave to simmer very gently for 20–25 minutes or until the vegetables are completely softened.

Discard the bay leaf, then purée the soup in a blender or food processor, with the crème fraîche or single cream. Thin with the milk. Season to taste, and reheat gently.

CROUTONS ˅

Add croutons to soups for extra texture or for a more filling meal. Using garlic makes the croutons even tastier.

Remove crusts from 4 slices of bread and cut into tiny cubes. Heat vegetable oil gently in a frying pan and fry the bread cubes over a medium heat, shaking to turn them until they begin to turn golden and become crisp. Add 1 clove of crushed garlic towards the end of cooking, keeping the heat down to prevent the garlic from burning. Stir the garlic croutons thoroughly. When evenly browned (be careful not to overcook them) remove the croutons from the pan with a slotted spoon and drain on kitchen paper.

Keep warm in a very low oven until ready to use.

LIGHT MEALS AND SIDE DISHES

HERE YOU'LL FIND AN EXCITING RANGE OF SNACKS, STARTERS AND SIDE DISHES THAT YOU CAN MAKE QUICKLY AND EASILY — FROM TEMPTING NIBBLES SUCH AS CRISP AND SUCCULENT CHEESE PALMIERS, TO CLASSIC DISHES LIKE VEGETABLE TEMPURA, WHICH ALWAYS LOOKS SO AMAZING.

MELTING AUBERGINES WITH SWEET PEPPERS

FOR 4

2 medium aubergines, cut into thick slices

sea salt

3 tbs olive oil

2 canned pimientos, drained and each cut into 4 pieces, or 1 large fresh red pepper, quartered and skinned (see page 13)

8oz (250g) soft goat's cheese or any soft cheese, sliced

freshly ground black pepper

stoned olives to garnish

This makes an excellent light lunch or supper dish, or you can serve it as a starter for a more formal meal. A glass of red wine and crusty wholemeal bread will complete the menu.

METHOD: Sprinkle the slices of aubergine with a touch of salt. Brush them with olive oil and place on a large baking tray. Bake at 220°C/425°F/gas 7 for 10–12 minutes or until soft and golden brown.

Layer the aubergine slices, pimientos and goat's cheese in four or eight stacks on a baking tray, seasoning with freshly ground black pepper as you go along. Top each stack with a piece of cheese. Return to the oven and bake for 5 minutes to heat through. Garnish with a stoned olive or two, and serve immediately.

LIGHT VEGETABLE TEMPURA

FOR 4

8oz (250g) courgettes, sliced thickly

8oz (250g) small button mushrooms

8oz (250g) broccoli florets

4oz (125g) cauliflower florets

vegetable oil for deep frying

For the batter:

4oz (125g) plain flour

1 free-range egg

7fl oz (200ml) water

large pinch of sea salt

Optional sauce:

4 tbs tamari sauce

grated fresh ginger and spring onion to taste

This tempura from Japan makes one of the best snack meals in the world. Lovely with a sweet and sour sauce (see page 87), the chilli dip (see page 89), or the tamari sauce here, and served with boiled rice.

METHOD: Prepare the vegetables. Put the batter ingredients into the blender or food processor and run it until smooth. It is ready to use.

Make the sauce you intend to use. Set aside.

Pour the oil about 3 inches (7.5 cm) deep into a large saucepan. Heat to 170°C/325°F.

Dip the pieces of vegetable into the batter one at a time and place carefully in the hot oil. Do not fry too many pieces at once. Fry the vegetables, turning them over occasionally, until they are lightly golden all over – each batch takes a couple of minutes. Lift out and put on to kitchen paper to drain. Keep these pieces hot in a warm oven while you fry the next batch. When all are fried, serve without delay.

PARTY EGGS

FOR 6

6 free-range eggs

5 tbs bottled or home-made mayonnaise (see page 86)

1 tsp mild mustard or more to taste

2 tbs sweet cucumber relish (optional)

sea salt and freshly ground black pepper

paprika

To garnish:

stoned olives, sliced, or capers

sprigs of parsley

You can vary the flavours in this recipe by using different relishes – sweetcorn or tomato for example – and curry powder instead of paprika. Feel free to improvise!

METHOD: Hard-boil the eggs for 10 minutes. Drain the eggs and plunge into cold water. Leave to cool.

When the eggs are cold, peel them carefully. Cut in half lengthwise and scoop out the yolks into a bowl. Mash the yolks with the mayonnaise, mustard, and relish if using. Season to taste with salt, pepper and paprika.

Pile the mixture back into the egg whites. Arrange on a plate and garnish with olives or capers and sprigs of parsley.

AUBERGINE CAVIAR ⌄

FOR 4

2 large aubergines

juice of 2-3 lemons

2½ tbs tahini (sesame paste)

3 tbs sesame seeds

1 large clove garlic, crushed

sea salt

4 tbs chopped parsley

1 tbs olive oil

This Middle Eastern dip is also known as 'poor man's caviar', although it is just as luxurious as the real thing. Serve with toasted triangles of pitta bread or carrot sticks.

METHOD: Pierce the aubergines several times with a sharp knife. Bake at 190°C/375°F/gas 5 for 30–40 minutes or until soft. Set aside to cool for about 30 minutes.

Peel the aubergines and discard the skin. Put the flesh in a bowl and immediately add the lemon juice. Mash well, or blend in the food processor. Add the tahini, sesame seeds and garlic and mix in thoroughly. Season with salt.

Spoon into a serving dish, cover and chill. To serve, sprinkle with parsley and drizzle with olive oil.

LIGHT SAUSAGE ROLLS v

MAKES 8

8 small vegetarian sausages

8 sheets filo pastry

olive oil

8 slivers firm cheese

These are so satisfying that any would-be
meat eaters will love them!

METHOD: Grill or fry the vegetarian sausages as instructed
on the packaging. Leave to cool.

Cut each sheet of filo pastry in half. Brush the pieces of
filo with olive oil and fold each one in half. Brush with oil
again. Roll up a sausage and a sliver of cheese in a folded
piece of filo, then roll up each roll in the remaining folded
pieces of filo. Brush the tops of the rolls with more olive oil
and place on a greased baking sheet. Bake at 200°C/400°F/
gas 6 for 20 minutes or until golden.

CHEESE PALMIERS

MAKES 20

*8oz (250g) frozen or
home-made puff pastry
(see page 104)*

*8oz (250g) Cheddar cheese,
grated*

paprika

These light cheese-filled pastries just melt in the
mouth. Perfect as an appetizer to nibble
before a meal, you will find that they disappear
like the melting snow.

METHOD: Roll out the pastry thinly into an oblong. Cover
thickly with the cheese and press it down well. Sprinkle
generously with paprika.

Fold one long edge of the pastry into the centre. Moisten
the upper side of the edge with water. Fold the other long
edge into the centre and press down to seal the edges
together. Cut across into ¼ inch (0.5 cm) slices. Lay them,
cut-side down, on a well-greased baking tray.

Bake at 220°C/425°F/gas 7 for 20 minutes or until golden
brown. Cool on a wire rack for 5 minutes, then serve.

CRISP FILO MUSHROOM PARCELS v

MAKES 24

7oz (200g) filo pastry

olive oil

24 tiny button mushrooms

Serve these irresistible morsels on cocktail sticks
as a nibble to go with drinks.

METHOD: Leave the sheets of filo pastry stacked. Cut the stack into 4 inch (10 cm) squares, then separate them; you need 24 squares. Brush each square with olive oil and place a tiny mushroom in the centre. Fold the filo around the mushroom to make a parcel. Brush the outside with more olive oil.

Bake on a metal baking sheet at 200°C/400°F/gas 6 for 20 minutes or until crisp and golden. Leave to cool for at least 5 minutes before serving.

FILO CHEESE STRAWS

MAKES 12–14

4oz (125g) filo pastry

olive oil

6oz (175g) cheese, finely grated

freshly ground black pepper

These 'cigars' are a variation on the theme
of cheese straws, and they really are irresistible, so
you probably need to make more than you
expect! Use a cheese with a good, strong flavour.

METHOD: Cut the filo sheets in half crosswise. Brush each one with olive oil, then fold in half and brush with oil again. Place a narrow band of grated cheese along one long edge and grind black pepper over the top. Roll up tightly. Cut the roll in half and brush the top with olive oil. Repeat with the remaining filo sheets. Place on a greased baking sheet and bake at 220°C/425°F/gas 7 for 15 minutes. Eat hot, or while still warm from the oven.

OPPOSITE: Crisp Filo Mushroom Parcels

MUSHROOM TRIANGLES

MAKES 4

2 tbs olive oil

3½ oz (100g) shallots, chopped

2-3 cloves garlic, crushed

8 oz (250g) mushrooms, sliced

2 tbs dry white wine

7 fl oz (200ml) double cream

7 fl oz (200ml) milk

1 oz (30g) cornflour

2 tbs chopped fresh basil or tarragon

sea salt and freshly ground black pepper

4 sheets filo pastry

melted butter

beaten egg to glaze

Crisp golden brown parcels of filo pastry contain a creamy mushroom mixture that is flavoured with garlic and fresh herbs.

METHOD: Heat the oil in a large saucepan and cook the shallots gently, covered, for 5 minutes or until soft. Add the garlic and mushrooms and cook for a further 8–10 minutes, uncovered and stirring occasionally. Add the wine and boil until it has evaporated, then stir in the cream. Bring to the boil and boil gently for 5 minutes.

Mix the milk with the cornflour, then add to the pan and bring back to the boil, stirring well. The mixture should be very thick. Remove from the heat and stir in the basil or tarragon. Season to taste. Leave to cool.

Cut one sheet of filo in half lengthways. Brush one filo strip with melted butter and set the other strip on top. Brush with butter again. Spoon one-quarter of the mushroom mixture on to one end of the layered filo strip. Bring one corner up over the filling and press it on to the opposite side of the strip, to make a diagonal fold. Press the edges together to seal. Flip this triangle shape up on the pastry strip. Continue flipping the triangle over and over, to the end of the strip. Fill and shape three more triangles in the same way.

Put the mushroom triangles on a baking sheet and brush them with beaten egg. Bake at 220°C/425°F/gas 7 for 8–10 minutes or until the pastry is crisp and golden brown. Serve warm, with dips.

VEGETABLE PURÉES

FOR 6

2 lb (1 kg) broccoli, trimmed and chopped

¼ pint (150 ml) crème fraîche or single cream

2 tbs soured cream

2 oz (50 g) cheese, grated

½ tsp each grated nutmeg and freshly ground black pepper

sea salt

You can adapt this basic recipe that uses broccoli to make many other vegetable purées, such as carrot, Brussels sprout, cauliflower, courgette, pumpkin, potato with celeriac, parsnip, cabbage and swede.

METHOD: Steam the broccoli for 8–10 minutes or until tender. Put it into a food processor with the crème fraîche or single cream and purée thoroughly, or press through a sieve. Stir in the soured cream and grated cheese. Add the nutmeg and pepper, and salt to taste.

LEEK AND POTATO PURÉE: Cook 1½ lb (750 g) potatoes, peeled, and 6 large leeks, sliced, in separate pans of boiling salted water until tender. Drain well, reserving the cooking liquid from the leeks. Soften 2 cloves garlic, sliced finely, in 3 tbs olive oil; add the leeks and cook gently for 10 minutes. Meanwhile, purée the potatoes in a blender or food processor with ¼ pint (150 ml) crème fraîche or single cream (vegans can use tofu instead). Add the leek and garlic mixture and run the machine again until the purée is completely smooth, adding some of the reserved leek cooking liquid to thin to the desired consistency. Season to taste, and reheat gently before serving.

CREAMED SPINACH PURÉE: Steam 2 lb (1 kg) fresh spinach, trimmed, until tender, then drain well, pressing out all excess liquid. Chop the spinach finely or work in a food processor until quite fine. Heat 1 tbs butter or olive oil in a pan, add the spinach and heat through, stirring. Stir in ¼ pint (150 ml) crème fraîche or single cream. Season to taste and serve.

MAIN COURSES

WHEN IT COMES TO THE MAIN COURSE, SOME PEOPLE STILL FEEL THAT A VEGETARIAN DISH IS NOT AS SUBSTANTIAL AS A MEAT ONE. MEAT SUBSTITUTES HAVE BEEN ADDED TO SOME OF THE RECIPES IN THIS CHAPTER, BUT THEY CAN EASILY BE OMITTED AS THESE DISHES ARE DELICIOUS IN THEIR OWN RIGHT.

LANCASHIRE HOT POT WITH BUTTER BEANS v

FOR 6

1 lb (500g) vegetarian steak chunks

vegetable oil

12 oz (350g) onions, sliced

1 lb (500g) potatoes, peeled and sliced

1 x 14 oz (400g) can butter beans, drained (or equivalent cooked dried, see page 106)

1 tbs dried mixed herbs

sea salt and freshly ground black pepper

1½–2 pints (900ml–1.2 litres) vegetable stock

Long slow cooking brings out all the flavours of the ingredients in this hot pot to perfection, and fills the kitchen with wonderful appetizing smells.

METHOD: Brown the steak chunks in a little oil. Layer the steak chunks, onions, potatoes and butter beans in a casserole. Season as you go with the herbs, lots of pepper and a little salt. Pour in the stock.

Cover the casserole tightly with a lid and cook at 200°C/400°F/gas 6 for 30 minutes. Turn the heat down to 170°C/325°F/gas 3 and cook for another 30 minutes. Allow to cool a little before serving, with steamed vegetables such as cauliflower, broccoli or leeks.

BAKED SWEETCORN PUDDING

FOR 3–4

1½ oz (40g) margarine

1 onion, chopped finely

1 large clove garlic, crushed

1 oz (25g) plain flour

1 tsp ground mace (optional)

¼ pint (150ml) skimmed or soya milk

1 x 14oz (400g) can sweetcorn, drained

1 x 4oz (125g) can mild chillies, drained and chopped

½ tsp sea salt

freshly ground black pepper

3 free-range eggs, beaten

Save this savoury pudding hot or warm.
Adding canned mild chillies is a delicious touch.

METHOD: Melt the margarine in a saucepan and cook the onion and garlic over a gentle heat, covered with a lid, for 10 minutes or until quite soft, stirring from time to time. Sift the flour with the mace, if using, then stir into the softened vegetables. Gradually add the milk, stirring all the time. When smoothly blended, cook gently for 1 minute.

Remove from the heat and stir in the sweetcorn, the optional chillies, the salt and pepper to taste. Stir in the beaten eggs. Pour into a greased 8–9 inch (20–22.5 cm) soufflé dish or other deep baking dish. Bake at 180°C/350°F/gas 4 for 40–45 minutes or until the centre of the pudding is just set.

YORKSHIRE PUDDINGS

MAKES 12

8oz (250g) plain flour, sifted

¼ tsp sea salt

2 free-range eggs

1 pint (600ml) skimmed or soya milk

vegetable oil for the tins

Yorkshire puddings are very simple to make
in the blender. Always leave the batter to stand
for an hour before using.

METHOD: Put the ingredients into the blender and blend until the batter is smooth. Leave to stand for 1 hour.

Pour a little oil into each of 12 individual deep bun tins or American muffin tins and heat in the oven at 220°C/425°F/gas 7 for 3–4 minutes. Spoon the batter into the tins and return to the oven. Bake for 10 minutes, then turn the heat down to 190°C/375°F/gas 5 and bake for a further 15 minutes or until risen and golden brown. Serve as soon as possible.

TOAD IN THE HOLE

FOR 4–6

8oz (250g) plain flour

¼ tsp sea salt

2 free-range eggs

1 pint (600ml) skimmed or soya milk

6 large vegetarian sausages

4 tbs vegetable oil, plus extra for frying the sausages

Crisp, tasty sausages inside a cloud of light, golden batter makes irresistible and popular family food. Here is the meatless version of this classic recipe.

METHOD: Sift the flour with the salt and put into the blender with the eggs and milk. Blend to a smooth batter, and leave to stand for 1 hour.

Lightly brown the sausages in a frying pan.

Heat the 4 tbs vegetable oil in a 10 inch (25 cm) square baking pan at 220°C/425°F/gas 7 for 5 minutes. Place the sausages in the oil and pour the batter over the top. Return to the oven and bake for 15 minutes, then turn the heat down to 190°C/ 375°F/gas 5 and bake for a further 20 minutes or until the batter is cooked through and golden.

Serve with tomato sauce (page 151) or a salsa (page 152).

OVERLEAF: Meatless Loaf and Yorkshire Puddings, and Aubergine and Herb Casserole, served with Potato and Cabbage Mash, Gravy and Carrots

MEATLESS LOAF

FOR 6

1 lb (500g) vegetarian mince

1 onion, chopped and softened in a little olive oil

4-6oz (125-175g) button mushrooms, sliced

2oz (50g) fresh breadcrumbs

2 free-range eggs, beaten well

¾ pint (450ml) vegetable stock

1 tbs chopped mixed fresh thyme and sage

1–2 tsp ground mace, or 1 tsp chilli powder or ground allspice (optional)

2 tbs tomato purée

freshly ground black pepper

The art of the meatless loaf is to tailor it to your taste – add your family's favourite spices or herbs, plus chopped, cooked vegetables of your choice to ring the changes. Peas, celery, leeks, broccoli and sweetcorn will all give interesting tastes and textures to the basic loaf here. Instead of the stock, you can add a 14oz (400g) can of chopped tomatoes with their juices, to make a very moist and tomatoey-tasting loaf.

METHOD: Mix all the ingredients together in a large bowl, or blend in a food processor. Pack into a well-greased 2lb (1kg) loaf tin and bake at 180°C/350°F/gas 4 for 1 hour or until crisp on top and set through. Leave to cool in the tin for at least 15 minutes before turning out. If you are cooking ahead of time, loosen the edges after 15 minutes, and turn out when cold.

Serve with rich tomato sauce (see page 86) and Yorkshire puddings (see page 32).

CHILLIES

Chillies come from a large botanical family with many varieties. You see them in the shops in all sizes and colours – red, green, cream and even purple. The plump green jalapeño chilli is popular and used in many Mexican dishes. Chillies vary in strength so err on the side of caution: start with a little and then add to taste.

Dried chillies are a useful standby and can be very hot. Canned chillies, however, tend to be milder and are a truly delicious way of spicing. Beware of chillies in vinegar – they blow your head off.

CHILLI NON CARNE v

FOR 4

2 tbs olive oil

1 large onion, sliced finely

2 cloves garlic, crushed

1½ tsp chilli powder or to taste

8oz (250g) vegetarian mince

¾ pint (450ml) vegetable stock

1 x 14oz (400g) can chopped tomatoes

1 x 14oz (400g) can red kidney beans, drained

1-2 canned mild green chillies, drained and chopped

sea salt

The classic chilli con carne – made with vegetarian mince instead of meat! It can be served either with rice or with baked potatoes, and a tossed salad of your choice. Mexican corn bread is another delicious accompaniment.

METHOD: Heat the oil and sauté the onion for 3–4 minutes, then add the garlic, chilli powder and mince and stir until well mixed. Brown for 5 minutes, stirring. Add the stock and the tomatoes with their juice, then leave to simmer gently, covered, for 20 minutes.

Add the kidney beans and the optional chilli and simmer for a further 15 minutes.

Season to taste, and leave to stand for 10 minutes before serving to allow the flavours to develop.

NOODLE BAKE

FOR 4

8oz (250g) egg noodles

½ pint (300ml) soured cream

6oz (175g) cottage cheese

5oz (150g) Cheddar cheese, grated finely

4fl oz (125ml) skimmed or soya milk

1 tbs chopped mixed fresh herbs

1 tbs chopped chives

sea salt and freshly ground black pepper

An easy to make and unusual version of macaroni cheese, this nutritious bake is seasoned with fresh herbs.

METHOD: Cook the noodles in boiling water, then drain and rinse under cold water. Mix together the soured cream, cottage cheese and 4oz (125g) of the Cheddar and stir in the milk. Add the herbs and season to taste. Mix thoroughly into the noodles.

Grease an 8inch (20cm) soufflé dish or other deep baking dish. Tip the noodle mixture into it and sprinkle the remaining Cheddar cheese on top. Bake at 180°C/350°F/ gas 4 for 20–25 minutes. Serve hot.

OMELETTES

An omelette is one of the simplest and quickest dishes ever. Leave it plain and serve with vegetables or a salad, or add a filling.

FOR 1

2 free-range eggs

sea salt and freshly ground black pepper

½ oz (15 g) margarine, or 2 tbs olive oil

FILLINGS:
mushrooms sautéed with garlic and parsley, grated cheese, masses of chopped fresh herbs with croutons if you like, sliced tomatoes sautéed in olive oil, boiled sliced new potatoes with chives – and so on.

METHOD: Beat the eggs until frothy, and season to taste. Melt the margarine, or heat the oil, in a small frying pan over moderate heat. When hot but not smoking, pour in the eggs, moving the mixture around a little to start with. When the surface begins to bubble, lift the cooked edges and allow the uncooked egg to run underneath. When the base of the omelette is lightly browned, fold in half. Cook a little longer so that the middle sets, and then flip on to a warm plate to serve.
• For a filled omelette, put the filling into the centre while the base is browning, then fold and cook a minute longer.

MEATLESS MEATBALLS WITH SAUCES

These are crisp on the outside and fine and smooth inside, and are quite delicious with a wild mushroom sauce (see page 87).

MAKES 12

8 oz (250 g) vegetarian mince

1 onion, chopped finely

1 oz (25 g) Cheddar cheese, grated

2 tbs chopped fresh mixed herbs, or 1½ tsp dried herbs

1 oz (25 g) fresh breadcrumbs

2 free-range eggs, beaten

sea salt and freshly ground black pepper

ground mace and allspice

plain flour

vegetable oil

METHOD: Mix the vegetarian mince with the onion, cheese, herbs, breadcrumbs and eggs in the blender. Blend until the mixture is smooth and quite fine. Season to taste and add the mace and allspice

Form into small meatballs and roll in flour to coat lightly. Fry in hot oil over moderate heat until nicely browned all over. Drain on kitchen paper and serve hot.

OPPOSITE: Meatless Meatballs with Sauces

COTTAGE CRUNCH CASSEROLE

FOR 8

1 lb (500 g) vegetarian mince

2 free-range eggs, beaten well

¾ pint (450 ml) water

8 oz (250 g) leeks, chopped and cooked in boiling water for 10 minutes

6 oz (175 g) mushrooms, sliced

2 oz (50 g) walnut pieces, chopped

1 tsp each ground mace and allspice, or 1-2 tsp curry powder (optional)

few drops of Tabasco sauce (optional)

12 oz (350 g) courgettes, steamed and sliced

6 oz (175 g) mangetout, steamed

4 sun-dried tomatoes in oil, chopped finely

3 tbs chopped mixed fresh herbs, e.g. parsley, fennel, coriander, marjoram, tarragon

4 oz (125 g) mozzarella cheese, sliced

3 oz (75 g) Cheddar cheese, grated

This layered casserole is special enough to be the main dish for Christmas dinner, or for other holiday or special occasion menus. Serve with the cheese and parsley sauce on page 85 and lots of roasted vegetables. Cranberry sauce will be welcome too.

METHOD: Mix the mince with the beaten eggs and stir in the water. Allow to soak for 30 minutes, then purée in the blender until fairly smooth. Add the prepared leeks, mushrooms and walnuts and season with the optional spices and Tabasco. Don't add salt as the vegetarian mince is sufficiently salty.

Grease a large baking dish. Spread half of the mince mixture on the bottom. Layer the sliced courgettes, mangetout, tomatoes, herbs and mozzarella over the top, and cover with the rest of the mince mixture. Sprinkle the grated cheese over the top. Bake at 180°C/350°F/gas 4 for 1 hour.

FRESH AND HOME-DRIED HERBS

When herbs are in season – from late spring through summer – they can be used to impart wonderful flavours and fragrances to food. Fresh herbs make a distinct difference to cooked dishes, and they are delicious in salads. When fresh herbs are out of season or unavailable, dried herbs are an excellent substitute for fresh in soups, casseroles and meatless dishes.

If you grow your own herbs you can dry them quite successfully yourself. Pick them in the morning when they are at the height of their fragrance. You can then either lay them on paper in a warm place to dry out, or tie them into small bunches and hang them in a warm, dry place with plenty of air circulating around them. When brittle – after several days – strip them off their stalks and store in dark jars out of direct sunlight.

AUBERGINE AND HERB CASSEROLE

FOR 8

*3½ lb (1.5 kg) ripe plum
tomatoes, skinned (see page
59), or 2 x 1½ lb (700g)
cans plum tomatoes, drained*

8 tbs olive oil

1 large onion, chopped

2 tbs chopped garlic

6oz (175g) tomato purée

*1 tbs each chopped fresh
oregano, basil and thyme*

*2lb (1kg) aubergines, sliced
diagonally ¼ inch (0.5cm)
thick*

plain flour

*sea salt and freshly ground
black pepper*

*8oz (250g) mozzarella
cheese, sliced*

I made this recipe when I was a young girl,
and recently cooked it for Pierre Franey of the New
York Times on his 'Great Cooks' series. It is
best eaten with a tossed salad, and either plain pasta
or fresh bread, and goes down well with a
glass of red wine. (See photograph on pages 34–5.)

METHOD: Chop the fresh or canned tomatoes into small
cubes. Heat 1 tbs of the olive oil in a saucepan and sauté
the onion and garlic, stirring, for 1 minute. Add the chopped
tomatoes and the tomato purée, and then the herbs. Stir
well and bring to a simmer. Cover and cook over a very low
heat for 30 minutes.

Meanwhile, dredge the slices of aubergine in flour and
sauté them in the rest of the olive oil in a large pan over
moderate heat until lightly browned on both sides.

Season the tomato sauce. Pour a layer of sauce over the
bottom of a baking dish and cover with a layer of aubergine.
Continue making layers, finishing with a layer of aubergines.
Arrange the sliced mozzarella over the top. Bake at
180°C/350°F/gas 4 for 1 hour or until golden brown.

LAYERED VEGETABLE TERRINE

FOR 6

1¼ lb (625 g) cauliflower, steamed until tender

1¼ lb (625 g) carrots, steamed until tender

12 oz (350 g) spinach, cooked and thoroughly drained

6 tbs crème fraîche or single cream

2 tbs chopped fresh coriander

3 spring onions, chopped finely

2 tsp ground ginger or to taste

1 tsp grated nutmeg or to taste

sea salt and freshly ground black pepper

6 free-range eggs

6 oz (175 g) large mushrooms, sliced

Festival and party food par excellence, this beautiful three-coloured loaf makes a meal for special occasions. It takes a while to make, but repays you handsomely.

METHOD: In three separate operations, purée the cauliflower, carrots and spinach, adding 2 tbs crème fraîche or single cream to each. Season the cauliflower with the chopped coriander, the carrots with the spring onions and ginger, and the spinach with the nutmeg. Add salt and freshly ground black pepper to all three mixtures. Stir 2 beaten eggs into each mixture.

Grease a 2 lb (1 kg) loaf tin. Place the cauliflower mixture on the bottom and arrange a layer of half the sliced mushrooms on top. Cover with the carrot mixture and add a layer of the remaining mushrooms. Finally, pour the spinach mixture over the top. Place the tin in a baking tray of hot water and bake at 200°C/400°F/gas 6 for 50–60 minutes or until a sharp knife inserted into the centre comes out clean.

Allow to stand for at least 10–15 minutes before attempting to turn out. Run a knife around the edge of the terrine to loosen the sides, then invert on to a large plate and tap the base of the tin until the terrine comes out. Serve with a sauce of your choice (see pages 84–9).

EASY CAULIFLOWER DHAL v

FOR 4-6

8oz (250g) green lentils, soaked for 1-2 hours

1 large onion, sliced

2in (5cm) root ginger, bruised

1 tbs chopped parsley

1 fresh green chilli ·

3 cloves garlic, chopped finely

2 tbs olive oil

2 tsp each ground turmeric, coriander and cumin

1 cauliflower, cut into florets and cooked

sea salt

A lovely 'dry' dhal with gentle spicing, this Indian dish goes beautifully with Chinese egg fried rice (see page 54), some cucumber raita and a crisp green salad.

METHOD: Drain the lentils and put them into a saucepan with the onion, ginger, parsley and whole chilli. Cover with water, bring to the boil and simmer for 30 minutes.

Meanwhile, cook the garlic gently in the oil for 3-4 minutes or until soft, then stir in the ground spices. Toss the cauliflower florets in the spiced mixture until well coated, and season to taste with sea salt.

Drain the lentils, remove the ginger and chilli and mix thoroughly with the spiced cauliflower.

SIMPLE VEGETABLE CURRY v

FOR 3-4

1 large onion, sliced

2 cloves garlic, sliced

2 tbs olive oil

2 tbs Madras curry paste or to taste

6oz (175g) frozen peas, thawed

1 large potato, scrubbed and diced

8oz (250g) carrots, sliced

8oz (250g) courgettes, diced

4oz (125g) mushrooms, sliced

You can vary the vegetables for this 'dry' curry: leeks, cauliflower and broccoli are all delicious, as are French beans, mangetout or sweetcorn.

METHOD: Soften the onion and garlic gently in the oil over a low heat, covered with a lid, for 10 minutes. Stir occasionally. When they are soft add the curry paste and stir for a few moments, then add the prepared vegetables. Toss until they are all well coated with the curried onion mixture. Cover tightly with a lid and cook over a very low heat for 30-40 minutes or until the vegetables are tender. (This steams the vegetables, and their juices run so you don't need to add stock.)

Remove from the heat and allow to stand until you are ready to eat – this dish improves on resting. Serve with plain or fried rice, and naan bread.

CURRIED CHICK PEAS WITH ONIONS v

FOR 4

2 tbs olive oil

2 onions, thinly sliced

2 cloves garlic, crushed

2 tbs sesame seeds

1 tbs curry powder or to taste

sea salt

2 x 14oz (400g) cans chick peas

3 tbs fresh lemon juice

1 tsp tamari or light soy sauce

3 tbs chopped fresh parsley

freshly cooked rice to serve

A deliciously spicy dish which is simple to prepare, and very nutritious. Serve spooned over plain boiled rice or the saffron rice on page 57, with pitta bread or naan.

METHOD: Heat the oil in a large frying pan and cook the onion and garlic very gently, covered, for about 25 minutes or until meltingly soft and golden. Stir in the sesame seeds and curry powder. Season with salt. Cook uncovered for 5 minutes, stirring occasionally.

Drain the chick peas, reserving 4 fl oz (125 ml) of the liquid. Add the chick peas to the pan with the reserved liquid and cook, stirring frequently, until the chick peas are hot and almost all the liquid has evaporated.

Stir in the lemon juice, tamari and parsley. Serve hot, spooned over rice.

TASTY BEANBURGERS

MAKES 4

2 tbs olive oil plus more for frying burgers

1 onion, chopped finely

2 cloves garlic, sliced finely

1 tsp cumin seeds (optional)

2 tbs chopped parsley

1 x 14oz (400g) can black-eyed or cannellini beans, drained

2oz (50g) fresh breadcrumbs

1 free-range egg

pinch of chilli powder

sea salt and freshly ground black pepper

So quick and easy to prepare, these beanburgers make a scrumptious lunch. Put a little chopped salad or a slice of cheese inside each bap, and serve with grilled tomatoes.

METHOD: Heat the oil and soften the onion and garlic, covered, for 5–6 minutes. Add the cumin seeds and cook for a further 3 minutes. Off the heat stir in the parsley and the beans. Mash until smooth, or blend in the food processor. Stir in the breadcrumbs and then the egg, mixing thoroughly. Season to taste with chilli, salt and pepper.

Shape into four burgers and fry in hot, shallow olive oil for 3–4 minutes on each side or until lightly browned. Serve inside warm fresh baps, with a little chopped salad or a slice of cheese.

GOAT'S CHEESE AND DILL SOUFFLÉ

FOR 4

2oz (50g) margarine

2oz (50g) plain flour

½ pint (300ml) hot skimmed or soya milk

4oz (125g) soft goat's cheese or feta cheese, cut into small cubes

2 tbs chopped fresh dill

4 free-range eggs, separated

sea salt and freshly ground black pepper

Soufflés are very quick and easy to make once you master the basics, and there are infinite variations you can try.

METHOD: Melt the margarine in a small heavy saucepan and stir in the flour until smooth. Gradually add the hot milk and stir until smooth and thick. Simmer very gently for 3–4 minutes, then stir in the cheese and the dill. Off the heat, stir in the egg yolks and season.

Whisk the egg whites until very stiff, and fold carefully into the cheese mixture. Spoon into a well buttered 8 inch (20 cm) soufflé dish and bake at 200°C/400°F/gas 6 for 20–25 minutes or until well risen and golden on top, but still creamy in the middle. Serve immediately.

VEGETABLE SOUFFLÉ

FOR 4

1 tbs chopped spring onion or shallot

½ oz (15g) margarine

8 oz (250g) cooked cauliflower florets, cut small

For the soufflé base:

2 oz (50g) margarine

1½ oz (40g) plain flour

½ pint (300ml) hot skimmed or soya milk

pinch each of cayenne pepper and grated nutmeg

sea salt and freshly ground pepper

4 free-range eggs, separated

Cauliflower makes a particularly good soufflé, and there are of course endless variations on the theme. You can substitute other cooked vegetables such as spinach (6 oz/175 g) or courgettes, broccoli, asparagus, mushrooms or petits pois 8 oz (250 g), using this master recipe. Grated Cheddar cheese (3 oz/75 g) is another option.

METHOD: Soften the spring onion or shallot in the margarine, then toss in the cauliflower florets and cook gently for 2 minutes. Set aside.

To make the soufflé base, melt the margarine in a heavy saucepan and stir in the flour until smooth. Gradually add the hot milk and stir until smooth and thick. Season to taste with the spices, salt and pepper. Simmer very gently for 3–4 minutes. Off the heat, stir in the egg yolks, mixing well. Fold in the cauliflower mixture. Whisk the egg whites until very stiff, and fold carefully into the cauliflower mixture.

Spoon into a well-greased 8–9 inch (20–22.5 cm) soufflé dish and put into a 200°C/400°F/gas 6 oven. Turn the heat down to 190°C/375°F/gas 5 and bake for 25–30 minutes or until the soufflé is well risen and golden on top, but still a little creamy in the centre. Serve immediately.

PASTA, RICE AND POTATOES

PASTA, RICE AND POTATOES ARE MAJOR CORNERSTONES OF THE MEATLESS DIET, PROVIDING CARBOHYDRATE BALANCE TO THE VEGETABLE INGREDIENTS AS WELL AS SATISFYING BULK. THEY ARE ENDLESSLY VERSATILE, AND CAN BE USED TO MAKE MAIN MEALS AS WELL AS SIDE DISHES. THEY ARE CHEAP, TOO, AND ALWAYS AVAILABLE.

SPAGHETTI WITH OLIVE OIL AND GARLIC

FOR 2

2-3 large cloves garlic (or more according to taste), crushed

3 tbs olive oil

freshly ground black pepper

6oz (175g) spaghetti

freshly grated Parmesan, to taste (optional)

chopped fresh herbs such as parsley, basil and oregano, to taste

This is one of my favourites – it's so easy.
I use lots of garlic, which I love, and which is very good for you. Serve with a Caesar salad (see page 78) and some fresh bread.

METHOD: Stir the crushed garlic into the olive oil and add masses of freshly ground black pepper.

Cook the spaghetti in boiling water until 'al dente' (see page 50) and drain well. Mix the garlicky oil into the hot spaghetti, add Parmesan and herbs, and toss thoroughly. Serve immediately.

VEGETARIAN PARMESAN

Parmesan cheese is traditionally made using animal rennet, and is not suitable for vegetarians. However, there are now a few brands of Parmesan on the market made with vegetable agents. If you cannot find one, substitute finely grated vegetarian Cheddar cheese.

PASTA SHELLS WITH LEEKS AND COURGETTES

FOR 4

2-3 tbs olive oil

3 leeks, sliced finely

4 medium courgettes, sliced finely

12 oz (350g) pasta shells

4 oz (125g) soft goat's cheese or feta cheese, crumbled, or Cheddar cheese, grated

2 tbs chopped fresh basil

sea salt and freshly ground black pepper

cayenne pepper

2 oz (50g) sun-dried tomatoes in oil, sliced thinly

grated cheese to hand around

Tasty and looks great too. You can substitute your favourite pasta shapes for the shells. Serve a fresh tomato salad with some mixed salad leaves alongside.

METHOD: Heat the olive oil in a frying pan and toss in the leeks and courgettes to coat them. Turn the heat down, cover and cook over a low heat for 10–15 minutes or until very soft. Stir occasionally. At the same time, cook the pasta until 'al dente' (see below).

Stir the crumbled goat's cheese into the leeks and courgettes and cook until well amalgamated. Add the basil and season to taste with salt, pepper and cayenne. Toss into the hot, well-drained pasta and sprinkle the sun-dried tomatoes over the top. Serve immediately, with grated cheese to hand around.

HOW TO COOK PASTA

1. Bring water (3$\frac{1}{2}$ pints/2 litres per 8 oz/250g pasta) to the boil with 1 tsp olive oil in a large pan and add a generous pinch of sea salt.

2. Put the pasta into the water and bring back to the boil. Simmer over a moderate heat for the shortest cooking time recommended on the packet. Stir from time to time. Alternatively, put the pasta into the boiling water and bring back to the boil, then remove the pan from the heat and cover with a lid. Leave to stand off the heat for the cooking time recommended on the packet, stirring from time to time.

3. To test the pasta, lift out a piece on a long-handled fork or slotted spoon: it is done when it is tender but still firm to the bite ('al dente'). Never overcook pasta.

4. Drain it in a colander, shaking well to remove all excess water. Serve immediately.

TAGLIATELLE WITH MUSHROOM SAUCE

FOR 4

1 large onion, chopped

2 cloves garlic, sliced finely

2 tbs olive oil

1 lb (500g) mushrooms

2 tbs each chopped fresh parsley and tarragon

1 lb (500g) tagliatelle

7 fl oz (200ml) crème fraîche or single cream

squeeze of lemon juice

sea salt and freshly ground black pepper

freshly grated nutmeg

The lovely flavour of tarragon goes well with the gentle creamy taste of mushrooms. Serve with a tossed leaf salad and some bread on the side.

METHOD: Cook the chopped onion and garlic in the oil, covered, over a gentle heat for 8–10 minutes or until softened. Put the mushrooms in the blender or food processor and run it until they are very finely chopped (or else chop them very finely indeed by hand). Add them to the pan with the herbs and cook for a further 6–8 minutes. At the same time, cook the pasta until 'al dente' (see page 50).

Stir the crème fraîche or single cream into the sauce and heat through gently. Add the lemon juice and season to taste with salt, pepper and nutmeg. Mix into the tagliatelle and serve immediately.

SPINACH FUSILLI BAKE

FOR 3–4

1 lb (500g) spinach, steamed

¾ pint (450ml) béchamel sauce (see page 85)

sea salt and freshly ground black pepper

grated nutmeg

10 oz (300g) fusilli, cooked until 'al dente' (see page 50)

2 tbs olive oil

2 large cloves garlic, crushed

5 large tomatoes, sliced

2 oz (50g) Cheddar cheese, grated

The original combination of layers – spinach, garlicky pasta and sliced tomatoes topped with cheese – makes a memorable meal.

METHOD: When the spinach is cool enough to handle, squeeze it thoroughly dry. Mix into the béchamel and season to taste with salt, pepper and nutmeg. Cover the bottom of a baking dish with the mixture. Toss the well-drained pasta with the olive oil and garlic and spread over the spinach layer. Arrange the tomato slices over the top, in slightly overlapping layers, and season well. Sprinkle the grated cheese over the top. Bake at 180°C/350°F/gas 4 for 40–45 minutes or until browned.

PASTA TWISTS WITH SPINACH AND NUTS

FOR 4

1 tbs olive oil

3 spring onions, chopped

1-2 cloves garlic, crushed

8 oz (250 g) fresh young spinach, chopped finely

1 tbs chopped fresh or 1 tsp dried tarragon

12 oz (350 g) pasta twists

¼ pint (150 ml) crème fraîche or single cream

2 oz (50 g) walnut pieces or pecans, chopped

sea salt and freshly ground black pepper

Crème fraîche is soured pasteurized cream. It is lighter than double cream and gives a delicious taste to pasta sauces. It combines beautifully with the strong flavour of spinach and the crunchy texture of the nuts.

METHOD: Heat the olive oil in a frying pan or wok and soften the spring onions and garlic for 1–2 minutes. Add the chopped spinach and optional tarragon and stir-fry for 3–4 minutes. At the same time cook the pasta until 'al dente' (see page 50). Stir the crème fraîche and walnuts into the spinach mixture and season to taste. Heat through.

Pour the sauce over the hot, well drained pasta and toss gently. Serve with grated cheese to hand around.

MACARONI SPECIAL

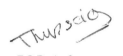

FOR 4–6

8 oz (250 g) macaroni

2 small leeks, shredded

2 free-range eggs

1 pint (600 ml) skimmed or soya milk

1 oz (25 g) margarine, melted, or 2 tbs olive oil

6 oz (175 g) Cheddar cheese, grated

sea salt and freshly ground black pepper

grated nutmeg

6 oz (175 g) mushrooms, sliced

This version of macaroni cheese is light and creamy, and makes wholesome, satisfying family food.

METHOD: Put the macaroni into a large pan of boiling water with the shredded leeks and simmer for 5 minutes or until half cooked. Drain.

Whisk the eggs with the milk and add the melted margarine or oil and the grated cheese. Season with salt, pepper and nutmeg.

Put the macaroni and leeks into a baking dish. Cover with the sliced mushrooms. Pour the egg mixture over the top and bake at 180°C/350°F/gas 4 for 35–45 minutes or until the top is browned. Leave for 10 minutes before serving, to allow it to set in the centre and cool a little.

WINTER LASAGNE

FOR 6

12 oz (350g) mushrooms, sliced

5 tbs vegetable oil

12 oz (350g) vegetarian mince

1 onion, chopped finely

1 x 1½ lb (700g) can tomatoes, drained and roughly chopped, or 1¼ lb (625g) fresh tomatoes, skinned (see page 13) and chopped

sea salt and freshly ground black pepper

crushed garlic to taste

dried mixed herbs

8 oz (250g) no-cook lasagne

1 lb (500g) fresh spinach, cooked and drained well then chopped

¾ pint (450ml) béchamel sauce (see page 85)

3 oz (75g) cheese, grated

2 free-range eggs, beaten

One of the joys of this dish is that it is so easy to prepare, especially when you use the lasagne that requires no pre-cooking. It can also be made well in advance and popped into the oven when you are ready to cook it. All it needs is a Caesar salad (see page 78) and warm granary bread.

METHOD: Sauté the mushrooms briskly in 3 tbs of hot oil until they are lightly cooked and crisp. Set aside. Mix the vegetarian mince with the chopped onion and cook in the rest of the oil for 4–5 minutes or until the onion softens.

Cover the bottom of an ovenproof dish with chopped tomatoes and season with salt and pepper, some crushed garlic and a sprinkling of dried mixed herbs. Cover with lasagne strips and make the next layer with the mince mixture. Season again. Spread spinach on top and then mushrooms. Continue making layers, finishing with a layer of lasagne.

Heat the béchamel gently and stir in the grated cheese until it melts. Remove from the heat and stir in the beaten eggs. Pour over the top of the lasagne, and bake at 190°C/375°F/gas 5 for 1 hour or until well browned on top.

CHINESE EGG FRIED RICE

FOR 6

1 tbs dark sesame oil

2 free-range eggs, beaten

1 tbs vegetable oil

4 spring onions, sliced finely

1 yellow pepper, deseeded and diced small

1 medium carrot, cut into fine matchsticks

8oz (250g) canned water chestnuts, sliced

4oz (125g) mangetout, sliced diagonally

1 inch (2.5cm) root ginger, peeled and grated

2 large cloves garlic, chopped finely

8oz (250g) long-grain rice, cooked (see below)

soy sauce

paprika

Although this is the ideal dish to go with samosas or spring rolls, or a simple stir-fry, it also makes an excellent main course in its own right. It is full of interest and colour, and the strips of lightly cooked free-range egg are a delicious finishing touch.

METHOD: Heat the sesame oil in a frying pan and pour in the beaten eggs. Stir a little until they set like a thin omelette, then flip over to cook the other side lightly. Turn out on to a wire rack and cool. Cut into thin strips.

Heat the vegetable oil in a wok until very hot. Stir-fry all the vegetables with the ginger and garlic for 3 minutes, then turn the heat down and cook for a further 3 minutes or until they are tender but still slightly crisp. Stir in the rice, mixing well, and season to taste with soy sauce and paprika. Finally, fold in the egg strips and it is ready to serve. Delicious with the sweet and sour sauce on page 87.

OPPOSITE: Simple Saffron Rice (top) see page 57 and Chinese Egg Fried Rice

---

HOW TO COOK RICE

There is a simple ratio of 1 to 2 when cooking rice: to one measure of rice you add two measures of water. So weigh the amount of rice required in the recipe, and put it into a cup or measuring jug. You will need two of the cups or measuring jugs full of water to cook the rice.

1. *Rinse rice before you cook it. Then put it into a saucepan, add the measured water and bring to the boil.*

2. *Turn the heat down and cover with a lid so that the pan is sealed. Leave the rice to cook, covered all the time, until it has absorbed all the water. This takes 8-10 minutes for white rice, or up to 20 minutes for brown or risotto rice.*

3. *Add some salt if you wish and fluff up the rice with a fork.*

GREEK RICE WITH LEEKS ᵥ

FOR 4

3 tbs olive oil

2 medium onions, chopped roughly

1 tsp chilli powder or to taste

6oz (175g) long-grain rice

½ pint (300ml) vegetable stock or water

12oz (350g) leeks, sliced

sea salt and freshly ground black pepper

thick plain Greek yogurt to serve (optional)

This tasty dish of chilli-spiced rice simmered gently with leeks is topped with thick Greek yogurt (which vegans can omit, of course).

METHOD: Heat the olive oil in a medium saucepan and sauté the onions for 3–4 minutes or until they begin to soften. Add the chilli powder and the rinsed rice and stir well to coat the grains with oil. Pour in the vegetable stock or water, stirring, then add the sliced leeks and a little salt and pepper. Bring to the boil. Turn the heat down and simmer gently, covered with a lid, for 20–25 minutes or until the rice is cooked. Check the seasoning.

Heap a tablespoon of thick Greek yogurt on top of each serving, if liked.

TYPES OF RICE

LONG GRAIN – *is the most versatile and popular of all types and comes white or brown.*

SHORT GRAIN – *is often used for risottos and puddings and is usually white. If you can find brown short-grain rice, use it to make delicious, slightly more crunchy risottos.*

BROWN RICE – *is the best rice in nutritional terms: the whole natural grain still with its edible husk, which makes it high in dietary fibre. It has a delicious flavour and nutty texture. Brown rice, both long-grain and short-grain, needs a little more water and longer cooking than white rice.*

BASMATI – *is a narrow long-grain rice variety with a fabulous flavour, great with Indian food. It comes brown or white. Grown in India and Italy.*

ARBORIO – *from Italy, is a plump short-grain rice with good flavour. It makes excellent risottos.*

'PUDDING' RICE – *is polished short-grain rice that goes mushy when cooked because of its high starch content. Perfect for a creamy rice pudding.*

WILD RICE – *is not a true rice at all, but the seed of a water grass. It is long and narrow, grey-brown in colour and nutty in flavour. Wild rice requires longer cooking than other rice – 30-40 minutes – but is nice to mix into rice dishes for variety. I always add a handful of wild rice to long-grain rice.*

RICE FLOUR – *is a good thickening agent in sauces and stews, and can be used in baking. Invaluable for people with a gluten allergy.*

PERSIAN CHILAU RICE ▾

FOR 4

6oz (175g) basmati rice

2 tsp ground cumin or to taste

sea salt

2 tbs olive oil

1oz (25g) margarine

To garnish:

thick plain Greek yogurt (optional)

toasted flaked almonds

An unusual way of cooking rice,
this has a crunchy texture and is gently spiced.

METHOD: Par-cook the rinsed rice for 5 minutes, then drain thoroughly. Mix with the cumin and a little salt.

Heat the olive oil with half of the margarine in a heavy-bottomed saucepan. Pack the rice into the pan, smooth the surface and dot with the remaining margarine. Cover closely with foil. Cover the pan tightly with a lid and turn the heat right down. Cook over the lowest possible heat for 35–40 minutes or until the rice is completely tender and a golden-brown crust has formed on the base. Season.

Spoon into a warm serving dish and top with a few spoonfuls of yogurt and toasted almonds.

SIMPLE SAFFRON RICE ▾

FOR 4

6oz (175g) basmati rice

2 tbs olive oil

2 fresh red chillies, deseeded and sliced very finely

3 cardamom pods, split open

1-2 tsp cumin seeds

3oz (75g) frozen peas, thawed

pinch of saffron strands soaked in 2 tbs water, drained

sea salt

1 cinnamon stick, bruised

2oz (50g) cashew nuts, browned lightly under the grill

Saffron yellow adds visual appeal to the flavour
of the spices in this rice dish, and
toasted cashew nuts provide a contrasting crunch.
See photograph on page 55.

METHOD: Rinse the rice and cook it until tender (see page 54). Meanwhile, heat the oil and toss the sliced chillies, cardamom pods and cumin seeds for about 2 minutes or until they give out their aromas.

Toss the spice mixture, peas and saffron into the drained hot rice and season with a little salt. Place the cinnamon stick in the centre and sprinkle the toasted cashew nuts over to garnish.

MUSHROOM RISOTTO

FOR 4

1 lb (500 g) mixed mushrooms, eg chestnut, shiitake, flat, field etc, sliced

4 tbs olive oil

2 cloves garlic, crushed

2 tbs chopped parsley

1 onion, chopped

6 oz (175 g) arborio or other risotto rice

2¼ pints (1.5 litres) hot vegetable stock

3 oz (75 g) cheese, grated

1 tbs finely chopped fresh tarragon

ground mace

sea salt and freshly ground black pepper

The delicate flavours of this risotto can be varied by adding chopped pumpkin or other vegetables. It is a delicious supper dish, perfect with a salad of mixed leaves dressed in the lemony caper vinaigrette on page 83.

METHOD: Sauté the mushrooms briskly for just a minute or so in 2 tbs of the olive oil, adding the crushed garlic and chopped parsley once the juices begin to run. Draw off the heat, cover with a lid and set aside.

Soften the onion in the rest of the oil over a gentle heat, covered, for 6–7 minutes. Then add the rice and stir until it is well coated with oil. Add a ladleful of the hot stock and simmer, stirring, until it has been absorbed, then add another ladleful of stock. Continue adding the stock a little at a time and simmering until the rice absorbs the liquid before adding more.

When all the stock has been added and the rice is fully cooked, stir in the cheese and tarragon. Season with mace, salt and pepper, fold in the mushrooms with all their juices, and serve.

SHEPHERD'S PIE ❧

FOR 4-6

1½ lb (750g) potatoes, peeled

3oz (75g) margarine

1-2 tbs skimmed or soya milk

sea salt and freshly ground
black pepper

1 large onion, chopped

2 carrots, sliced thinly

8oz (250g) vegetarian mince

2 tbs soy sauce

½ pint (300ml) vegetable
stock

ground mace, grated nutmeg
or garam masala (optional)

Nothing can beat a good shepherd's pie.
Making it with vegetarian mince is even better than
the original version because it is lighter.

METHOD: Cook the potatoes in boiling water for 20
minutes or until quite soft, then drain well and mash them
with 2oz (50g) of the margarine and enough skimmed or soya
milk to make a firm but smooth consistency. Season to taste.

Melt the remaining margarine in a frying pan and add
the onion and carrots. Cover with a lid and cook for about
10 minutes or until soft, stirring occasionally. Add the
vegetarian mince, soy sauce and vegetable stock. Bring to the
boil and simmer gently, uncovered, for 8–10 minutes. Season
to taste with salt and pepper and any spices of your choice.

Put the mince mixture into a baking dish and cover with
the mashed potatoes. Bake at 200°C/ 400°F/gas 6 for 30
minutes or until the potato topping is well browned.

GARLIC MASHED POTATOES ❧

FOR 3-4

4 cloves garlic

½ tsp sea salt

6 tbs olive oil

squeeze of lemon juice

2lb (1kg) potatoes, freshly
boiled

freshly ground black pepper

Garlic lovers, this is a sensational way of
eating potatoes – and garlic! It is based on a simple
Spanish sauce of pounded garlic and olive oil.

METHOD: In a mortar pound the garlic to a fine paste with
the salt. Add the oil in a slow stream, pounding all the time
so that the sauce thickens. Add the lemon juice to thin out
the sauce and season with more salt if necessary.

Mash the hot potatoes well, then gradually beat in the
garlic oil with an electric mixer or whisk. Season with
pepper, and serve.

CREAMY POTATO AND LEEK BAKE

FOR 2-3

2 large cloves garlic, crushed

2 tbs olive oil

8oz (250g) mushrooms, sliced

2 tbs chopped fresh herbs, eg thyme, tarragon and parsley, or 1½ tsp dried mixed herbs, plus more for the layers

12oz (350g) potatoes, peeled and sliced thinly

12oz (350g) leeks, sliced

sea salt and freshly ground black pepper

grated nutmeg

6fl oz (175ml) crème fraîche or single cream

5 tbs skimmed or soya milk

2oz (50g) fresh breadcrumbs

1oz (25g) margarine

Layers of thinly sliced potatoes and leeks, with a central layer of mushrooms flavoured with garlic and fresh herbs, are baked under a creamy topping with crisp crumbs.

METHOD: Sauté the garlic in the oil for 2 minutes, then add the mushrooms and herbs and toss together. Cover and cook gently for 5 minutes.

Layer half of the potatoes and leeks in an ovenproof dish and season with salt, pepper, nutmeg and a sprinkling of herbs. Spoon the mushrooms and all their juices over the top and cover with the rest of the leeks and potatoes. Spoon the crème fraîche or cream over the top and add the skimmed or soya milk. Cover tightly with foil and cook at 190°C/375°F/gas 5 for 1 hour.

Remove the foil. Sprinkle over the breadcrumbs, dot with the margarine and bake, uncovered, for 25–30 minutes or until the potatoes are tender.

PEELING GARLIC

Press down on the clove with the flat side of a knife blade, then pull away the burst skin.

POTATO AND CABBAGE MASH v

FOR 3–4

1 lb (500g) boiled potatoes

¼ pint (150ml) skimmed or soya milk

1 lb (500g) cooked green cabbage, chopped

6 spring onions, sliced finely

pinch of grated nutmeg

sea salt and freshly ground black pepper

melted margarine

Here is a traditional country dish devised just for cold, bleak winter weather.

METHOD: Mash the potatoes with the milk, or blend them together in the food processor. Turn into a saucepan and reheat, stirring. Add the cabbage and spring onions and mix well. Season with nutmeg, salt and pepper. Heat through.

Put into a dish, or place piles of mash on each plate, and make a deep well in the centre. Fill the well with melted margarine to dip each forkful of mash into.

SAUTÉ OF SWEET POTATOES v

FOR 2–3

4 medium sweet potatoes, peeled

1½ oz (40g) margarine

grated rind and juice of 1 orange

4 oz (125g) brown sugar

2 tbs chopped fresh parsley or chives

Sweet potatoes are loaded with beta carotene. Boil them in the same way as ordinary potatoes, as in this recipe. You can also bake them in their jackets (they don't take as long as ordinary potatoes), roast them, or make them into chips to serve with soured cream.

METHOD: Cook the sweet potatoes in boiling water for 10–15 minutes or until they are tender. Drain well. Slice them or cut into cubes.

Heat the margarine in a frying pan and add the sweet potatoes. Toss over a moderate heat until the potatoes are covered with margarine, then add the orange rind and juice, the sugar and herbs. Heat through, stirring and tossing, and serve immediately.

STUFFED BAKED POTATOES

FOR 4–6

4 large baking potatoes, scrubbed

½ pint (300 ml) béchamel sauce (see page 85)

4 oz (125 g) Cheddar cheese, grated, plus more for the tops

4 oz (125 g) cooked peas

4 oz (125 g) cooked carrots, diced small

A nice change from plain jacket potatoes. You can vary the filling – chopped onions or leeks, sliced mushrooms, diced peppers and sweetcorn would all be delicious.

METHOD: Bake the potatoes at 200°C/400°F/gas 6 for 1¼ hours or until tender. Cut in half lengthwise and remove the flesh, being careful not to break the skins. Put the flesh in a bowl and set the skins aside.

Heat the béchamel gently and stir in the grated cheese until it melts. Add to the potato flesh and mash well, then fold in the prepared vegetables. Fill the potato skins with the mixture. Cover with more grated cheese and replace in the oven. Bake for a further 6–8 minutes or until the tops are lightly browned.

SPICY BEAN JACKETS v

FOR 2

2 baking potatoes, scrubbed

1 tbs olive oil

1 small onion, chopped

1 x 14 oz (400 g) can baked beans

2 tbs curry paste or to taste

An easy lunch or supper dish, this will be very popular with both children and adults. In cold weather, serve bowls of soup too.

METHOD: Bake the potatoes at 200°C/400°F/gas 6 for 1¼ hours or until tender. Alternatively, microwave them for 10 minutes on full power.

Heat the oil in a pan and sauté the onion for 5–6 minutes or until crisp and browned. In another pan, heat the baked beans with the curry paste.

Cut the potatoes in half lengthwise. Cut a deep cross in the flesh of each half and top with the spiced baked beans. Sprinkle with the browned onions and serve.

SAVOURY FRIED POTATO v

FOR 2-4

1 lb (500 g) mashed potatoes

plain flour

sea salt

freshly ground black pepper

vegetable oil

margarine

This is a delicious way to use up left-over mash!
You can vary the recipe with sautéed
mushrooms, leeks or onions, or grated cheese.

METHOD: Divide the mashed potatoes into 4 or 8 equal
portions and shape each into a cake with floured hands. (If
the potatoes are moist you will need to mix a bit of flour
into them to help bind the cakes.) Season some flour and
use to coat the cakes lightly.

Heat a mixture of oil and margarine in a frying pan and
fry the cakes over a moderate heat until crisp and golden
brown on both sides. Serve hot.

CRISPY POTATO SKINS v

FOR 4

4 baking potatoes, scrubbed

sunflower or grapeseed oil

sea salt

These make a very healthy snack, a good
alternative to potato crisps. You can serve them
with the chilli dip on page 89 or guacamole
(see page 88), or any other favourite dip or salsa.

METHOD: Bake the potatoes at 200°C/400°F/gas 6 for
1¼ hours or until tender. Alternatively, microwave them for
10 minutes on full power. Leave to cool a little, then cut in
half and carefully scoop out the flesh (you can use this for
mashed potato or shepherd's pie, see page 60). Cut each
half skin into three wide strips and then into squares.

Heat some oil in a frying pan until it is very hot – when
you drop the first potato skin into the oil it should
immediately start to sizzle. Cook the skins quickly on both
sides until golden and crisp. Drain on kitchen paper to
absorb excess oil, sprinkle with a little salt, and they are
ready to serve.

OPPOSITE: Sauté of Sweet
Potatoes, and Crispy Potato
Skins with a yogurt and
lemon dip

PASTRY

PASTRY DISHES ALWAYS LOOK SO APPETIZING — CRISP, GOLDEN AND MOUTHWATERINGLY LIGHT. THIS WONDERFUL SELECTION OF RECIPES DEMONSTRATES JUST HOW VERSATILE PASTRY IS, FROM THE ELEGANT FILO AND PUFF PASTRY TO EVER-POPULAR PASTIES.

CHEESE AND BROCCOLI TART

FOR 6

9oz (275g) easy shortcrust pastry (see page 103)

1 large onion, chopped

1 tbs olive oil

12oz (350g) broccoli florets

sea salt and freshly ground black pepper

4oz (125g) goat's cheese, sliced

4 free-range eggs

¼ pint (150ml) skimmed milk or single cream

3-4 tbs skimmed or soya milk

This distinctive tart, with the tangy flavour of goat's cheese, makes a memorable lunch, or is excellent on a picnic. You can use ricotta or Cheddar if you prefer a softer taste, and you can substitute cauliflower for broccoli as a variation.

METHOD: Roll out the pastry dough and line a greased 9–10 inch (22.5–25 cm) loose-bottomed flan tin. Bake blind until part cooked.

Soften the onion in the oil, covered for 5 minutes. Steam the broccoli florets for 5–6 minutes or until tender but still slightly crisp. Mix them with the onion and season with salt and pepper. Spread in the bottom of the cooked pastry case with the slices of cheese.

Beat the eggs thoroughly and stir in the milk or cream plus the extra milk. Season to taste. Pour over the broccoli. Bake at 200°C/400°F/gas 6 for 30 minutes or until lightly browned and set. Serve hot or warm.

MUSHROOM FILO PIE

FOR 4–6

2 shallots, sliced finely

3 tbs olive oil plus extra for the pastry

1½ lb (750g) mixed mushrooms, eg chestnut, shiitake, oyster, common and flat, all thinly sliced in the food processor

2 cloves garlic, crushed

3 tbs chopped parsley

2 tbs chopped fresh tarragon

5 tbs crème fraîche or single cream

3oz (75g) basmati rice, cooked (see page 56)

6oz (175g) filo pastry

A dramatic pie which makes a perfect party piece, this dish is full of flavour and texture – the succulence of mushrooms, the crispness of wafer-thin filo pastry, and a hint of smooth rice.
Serve with the wild mushroom sauce on page 87 and a garlicky salad.

METHOD: Soften the shallots in 1 tbs of the oil, then add the rest of the oil and the thinly sliced mushrooms. Toss until the mushrooms are well coated with oil and beginning to heat through, then turn the heat down a little and cover with a lid. Cook gently for 6–8 minutes or until the mushrooms are tender but not soggy, stirring occasionally. Add the garlic and herbs and stir well, then stir in the crème fraîche or single cream off the heat. Finally mix in the cooked rice and leave to cool.

Oil an 8 inch (20 cm) shallow tin, either square or round. Layer half of the filo pastry sheets in the tin, letting the edges of the pastry hang over the side of the tin all around by several inches. Brush each layer with oil as you go along. Drain excess liquid from the mushroom mixture, then spread it in the centre of the tin. Fold the pastry edges into the centre. Continue making layers with the rest of the filo, brushing with oil as you go, and crumpling, creasing or twisting up the top sheets to make a pattern. Brush the top well with more olive oil.

Bake at 200°C/400°F/gas 6 for 30 minutes or until golden. Cut into wedges and serve.

CREAMY VEGETABLE PIE

FOR 4–6

*8 oz (250g) sweetcorn, fresh
or canned*

12 oz (350g) broccoli

12 oz (350g) courgettes

12 oz (350g) carrots

4 oz (125g) French beans

3 small leeks

*½ pint (300ml) béchamel
sauce (see page 85), made
with ¼ pint (150ml) single
cream and ¼ pint (150ml)
milk*

*bunch of fresh summer herbs
of your choice, eg tarragon,
thyme, dill, chopped*

*8 oz (250g) frozen or home-
made puff pastry (see page
104)*

The joy of this pie is that you can make it across the
seasons, choosing your favourite vegetables.
It makes a mouthwatering meal, served with noodles
and the Caesar salad on page 78.

METHOD: Steam all the vegetables separately until they
are tender but still slightly crisp. Alternatively, cook them
in the microwave. Leave to cool, reserving cooking
liquids, then chop if necessary into bite-size pieces.

Thin out the béchamel with about ¼ pint (150 ml) of
the reserved liquids. Stir in the vegetables and herbs and
pour into a large ovenproof dish.

Roll out the pastry to a round or other shape that is
1 inch (2.5 cm) larger than the diameter of the dish. With
the trimmings make a long thin strip of pastry. Moisten
the rim of the dish and place this strip on it. Moisten the
strip, then place the pastry lid on top and press down
with a fork to seal the edge.

Bake at 200°C/400°F/gas 6 for 30–40 minutes or until
the pastry is risen and golden.

CLASSIC PASTIES ∨

MAKES 4

6 oz (175 g) vegetarian mince

4 oz (125 g) each potato, turnip and carrot, all grated finely

sea salt and freshly ground black pepper

1 lb (500 g) easy shortcrust pastry (see page 103)

4 tbs water

milk

Nothing could be easier or cheaper than these tasty pasties. Made in the classic way, they need a lot of tomato sauce to go with them, and are a very satisfying supper dish.

METHOD: Mix the vegetarian mince with the grated vegetables and season with salt and pepper. Roll out the pastry and cut into four 8 inch (20 cm) circles, or you can make 8 little pasties, using 5 inch (12.5 cm) circles. Divide the mince mixture among the circles, placing it in a heap in the centre. Add ½–1 tbs water to each. Moisten the pastry edges, then fold over into half-moon shapes. Press the edges together, turn them and crimp with a fork to make sure they are well sealed. Brush with milk and place on a well-greased baking tray.

Bake at 220°C/425°F/gas 7 for 10 minutes, then turn the heat down to 180°C/350°F/gas 4 and bake for a further 50 minutes. Cool a little on a rack, then lift carefully off the baking tray to serve.

LIGHT SPINACH AND CHEESE PIE

FOR 4

1 onion, chopped

1 tbs olive oil

1½ lb (750g) cooked spinach, well drained and chopped

¼ pint (150ml) béchamel sauce (see page 85)

4 oz (125g) Caerphilly cheese, grated

sea salt and freshly ground black pepper

grated nutmeg

9 oz (275g) easy shortcrust pastry (see page 179)

1 free-range egg yolk, beaten

This traditional pie makes a delicious meal served with potato and cabbage mash (see page 62). Good, honest, country food.

METHOD: Soften the onion in the oil for 5–6 minutes, covered with a lid. Add the spinach and mix well, then stir in the béchamel. Mix in the grated cheese. Season with salt, pepper and nutmeg. Set aside.

Roll out 5 oz (150g) of the pastry dough and line a greased 8 inch (20 cm) round tin, leaving a raised rim around the edge. Pour the spinach filling into the pastry case. Roll out the rest of the pastry dough into a round ½ inch (1 cm) larger in diameter than the top of the tin. Moisten the bottom pastry rim, place the top carefully over it and crimp the edges together tightly. Press them down with a fork to seal. Brush the top with beaten egg yolk.

Bake at 200°C/400°F/gas 6 for 30–35 minutes or until the pastry is golden. Serve hot or warm.

DEALING WITH ONIONS

Peeling pungent onions can make your eyes water, so rinse your hands frequently – it will reduce the effect of the onions.

Softening onions in oil or margarine, which is such a basic step in so many recipes, is best done by first tossing the sliced or chopped onions in the oil or fat over a moderate heat until well coated and then turning the heat down very low, covering the pan with a lid and leaving the onions to cook very gently for 10–12 minutes. They become very soft and sweet because this process steams them rather than browns them. Stir just once or twice during the cooking.

Browning onions is done over a higher heat – and they taste much stronger than onions softened by the method above.

SALADS

EATING FRESH, RAW INGREDIENTS HAS BEEN SHOWN TO BE BENEFICIAL TO HEALTH, AND IS RECOMMENDED AS PART OF THE DAILY DIET. YOU CAN EAT SALADS AS MAIN MEALS, AS STARTERS OR AS A SIDE DISH, EVEN IN WINTER. FULL OF VITAMINS AND MINERALS, SALADS GIVE US A FEELING OF VITALITY AND ENERGY THAT MANY OTHER FOODS DO NOT.

POTATO AND COS LETTUCE WITH GARLIC VINAIGRETTE v

FOR 4-6

2 large cloves garlic, crushed

5 tbs vinaigrette (see page 82)

2 lb (1 kg) new potatoes, scrubbed

1 cos lettuce, shredded coarsely

1 small red onion, chopped finely

chopped chives to garnish

The slightly bitter flavour of cos lettuce goes beautifully with the bland delicacy of potato, in a delicious garlicky dressing. Chopped chives are a perfect finishing touch.

METHOD: Stir the crushed garlic into the vinaigrette and leave to stand while you prepare the rest.

Cook the potatoes in boiling salted water until just tender but still firm in the centre. Drain, and rinse under cold water. Leave to cool, then cut into small cubes or slices.

Combine the potatoes, shredded cos and chopped onion in a salad bowl. Toss with the vinaigrette until well mixed and leave to stand for 20–30 minutes. Scatter chopped chives over the top just before serving.

SUN-DRIED TOMATO AND CHICK PEA SALAD ▾

FOR 4–6

½ small red onion, chopped finely

1 tbs white wine vinegar

4 tbs red wine vinegar

1 clove garlic, chopped finely

sea salt and freshly ground black pepper

2 tbs extra virgin olive oil

1 x 14oz (400g) can chick peas, drained (or equivalent cooked dried, see page 106)

2oz (50g) sun-dried tomatoes in oil, diced

2 tbs chopped fresh parsley or tarragon

2 tbs fresh lemon juice

A garlicky dressing and the sweet-sharpness of cooked red onion in vinegar give this unusual salad memorable qualities. Serve with warm pitta bread as a light lunch dish or a starter.

METHOD: Bring a small saucepan of water to the boil, add the onion and cook for 30 seconds. Drain, and toss with the white wine vinegar.

Mix together with the red wine vinegar, garlic, salt and pepper and gradually whisk in the oil. Toss the chick peas, sun-dried tomatoes and onion with the dressing and leave to marinate for 1 hour.

Add the chopped parsley or tarragon and lemon juice, toss to mix and serve at room temperature.

BEETROOT SALAD WITH SOURED CREAM AND GARLIC

FOR 4

1½ lb (750g) beetroot, cooked and skinned

¼ pint (150ml) soured cream

1 tbs fresh lemon juice

3 cloves garlic, crushed

freshly ground black pepper

1 tbs chopped fresh parsley or tarragon

A wonderful salad for winter, with rich flavours and beautiful colours – red, pink and green. Cooked beetroot are an excellent addition to many salads; here they play the starring role.

METHOD: Cut the prepared beetroot into medium-thin slices. Mix the soured cream with the lemon juice and garlic and season with pepper. Dress the beetroot, mixing gently until well coated. Pile into a salad bowl and sprinkle with the chopped parsley.

CAULIFLOWER SALAD WITH MUSTARD MAYONNAISE

FOR 4

2 medium potatoes, peeled and cubed

1 small cauliflower, cut into florets

2-3 tsp grainy mustard

3 tbs bottled or home-made mayonnaise (see page 86)

2 tbs fresh lemon juice

2 tbs plain set yogurt

1 tbs chopped fresh tarragon

2 stalks celery, sliced

chopped parsley to garnish

A simple salad with a distinctive flavour, this is excellent fare at any time of year, useful for a party or buffet table. It would go well with goat's cheese soufflé (see page 46) to make a light meal.

METHOD: Steam the potatoes until just tender. Steam the cauliflower florets for 4–5 minutes or until they are slightly cooked but still crunchy. Cool, and slice them.

Mix the mustard into the mayonnaise, add the lemon juice and stir in the yogurt and the tarragon. Toss the potato, cauliflower and celery gently with this dressing, and put into a dish. Sprinkle with the chopped parsley.

POTATO SALAD

FOR 4

1½ lb (750g) small waxy potatoes, peeled, or new potatoes, scrubbed

4 stalks celery, chopped

6 spring onions, sliced finely

2-3 tbs fresh lemon juice

5 tbs bottled or home-made mayonnaise (see page 86)

large handful of fresh dill, chopped

small bunch of parsley, chopped

1 dill-pickled cucumber, chopped (optional)

A delectable salad for all seasons: waxy potatoes, crunchy celery plus some spring onions in a lemony mayonnaise scented with dill and parsley.

METHOD: Cook the potatoes in boiling salted water until just tender but still firm in the centre. Cool, and cut into cubes. Mix with the celery and spring onions.

Add lemon juice to the mayonnaise, flavouring it so that it is quite sharp. Stir in the chopped dill and mix thoroughly. Toss the potatoes in the dressing until well coated.

Put into a salad bowl and garnish with chopped parsley and dill-pickled cucumber (if using).

TECHNICOLOUR BEAN SALAD ▼

FOR 6

2 x 14oz (400g) cans mixed beans (or equivalent cooked dried beans such as haricot, black-eyed, red kidney etc, see page 106)

8oz (250g) French beans, trimmed

6-8 spring onions, chopped finely

medium bunch of parsley, chopped finely

For the garlic dressing:

juice of ½ lemon

2-3 tbs wine vinegar

1 tsp sea salt

4 large cloves garlic, chopped finely

freshly ground black pepper

¼ pint (150ml) extra virgin olive oil

A bright salad with interesting flavours, this is tossed in a very garlicky vinaigrette. It makes an excellent addition to a buffet table, or it can be served as a starter or part of a light meal.

METHOD: To make the dressing, mix together the lemon juice, vinegar, salt and garlic in a bowl and add lots of freshly ground black pepper. Stirring all the time, dribble in the olive oil so that the dressing thickens as you work it. Check the seasoning.

Drain the canned beans and rinse them. Drain thoroughly. Steam the French beans for 5–6 minutes or until just tender. Toss all the beans together with the spring onions, then add the garlic dressing and toss again. Sprinkle the chopped parsley over the top. Serve at room temperature.

CAESAR SALAD

Deservedly a classic, Caesar salad can be served as a starter or side dish. It can be a light meal in itself, too, with just some warm wholemeal bread.

FOR 4

3 slices of bread, crusts removed

oil for frying

1 large crisp lettuce

3 oz (75 g) lamb's lettuce

8 spring onions, trimmed

3 tbs finely grated cheese

For the dressing:

2 tbs balsamic vinegar

1 tbs fresh lemon juice

1 tbs Dijon mustard

4 tbs extra virgin olive oil

1 large clove garlic, crushed

METHOD: Cut the bread into small cubes and fry in hot oil until crisp and golden all over. Drain and cool on kitchen paper. Mix together the ingredients for the dressing.

Divide the lettuce into leaves and tear larger leaves into manageable pieces. Put into a bowl with the lamb's lettuce and spring onions and sprinkle the cheese over the top. Toss the salad with the dressing and fold the croutons in just before serving.

CURRIED PASTA SALAD ▾

A main-dish salad with plenty of bite and zest. You can add chopped mango for an exotic touch, plus a garnish of fresh coriander leaves if you like.

FOR 4

12 oz (350 g) pasta shells

1 tsp extra virgin olive oil

8 oz (250 g) baby mushrooms

3 spring onions, chopped

2 stalks celery, sliced thinly

For the dressing:

1/4 pint (150 ml) extra virgin olive oil

4 tbs white wine vinegar

2 tbs fresh lemon juice

2 tbs light soft brown sugar

1 1/2 tbs curry powder

METHOD: Cook the pasta until 'al dente' (see page 50), then drain thoroughly and rinse under cold water. Toss thoroughly with the oil, mixing with your hands so that the pasta shells are separated. Add the mushrooms, spring onions and celery.

Mix together the dressing ingredients, add to the pasta salad and toss well. Refrigerate for 1 hour or overnight, but serve at room temperature.

PASTA AND BEAN SALAD WITH BASIL AND PECORINO

FOR 6

8 oz (250g) pasta bows

1 red pepper, skinned (see page 13) and cut into thin slices

1 yellow pepper, skinned (see page 13) and cut into thin slices

6 oz (175g) green beans, cooked

4 oz (125g) kidney beans (canned or cooked dried, see page 106)

3 tbs chopped parsley

¼ pint (150ml) vinaigrette (see page 82)

handful of fresh basil leaves, shredded

2 oz (50g) pecorino cheese, pared finely into shavings

An alluring mixture of peppers, green beans and kidney beans, pasta and herbs, this salad's finishing touch is finely pared cheese. It's really a meal in itself, served with warm fresh bread.

METHOD: Cook the pasta bows in boiling water until 'al dente' (see page 50). Drain, and rinse immediately under cold water in the colander.

Mix the peppers, pasta bows, green beans, kidney beans and parsley in a salad bowl, add the dressing and toss until thoroughly mixed together. Finally, fold in the basil and garnish with the pecorino shavings.

ORANGE RICE SALAD ∨

FOR 6

6oz (175g) long-grain rice

1 pint (600 ml) fresh orange juice

2 canned pimentos, drained and cut into strips

1 small red onion, chopped finely

4oz mangetout, trimmed and sliced

2 large oranges, peeled and divided into segments

7-8 tbs vinaigrette (see page 82)

The unusual method of cooking rice in orange juice gives it an exceptional flavour. A tasty mixture of pimientos and mangetout, plus some red onion, is added to the rice to make up an unusual and delectable salad.

METHOD: Rinse the rice and put into a saucepan with the orange juice. Bring to the boil. Stir once, then cover tightly and cook very gently for 15 minutes or until the liquid is absorbed and the rice tender. Fluff it up with a fork and leave to cool in a bowl.

Mix the prepared vegetables into the cooled rice. Cut up the orange segments and mix them in. Toss thoroughly with the vinaigrette, and it is ready to serve.

WARM GOAT'S CHEESE SALAD

FOR 4

1 crisp lettuce

2oz (50g) fresh young spinach leaves

1 bunch of watercress

a handful of small radicchio leaves

3 tbs vinaigrette (see page 82)

4 sun-dried tomatoes in oil, sliced finely

1 tbs chopped mild onion

6oz (175g) creamy goat's cheese

olive oil

This salad makes a lovely starter, especially served with hot garlic bread. Many goat's cheeses are made without the use of animal rennet, and will say so on the packet.

METHOD: Prepare all the salad leaves and toss them in the vinaigrette with the sun-dried tomatoes and onion. Divide among four plates. Slice the goat's cheese into rounds and brush them with olive oil. Grill until they blister and turn slightly golden, then place on top of the salads and serve immediately, with warm French bread.

OPPOSITE: Warm Goat's Cheese Salad

VINAIGRETTE v

FOR 4–6

1-2 tsp mild or grainy mustard

2 tbs fresh lemon juice

2 tbs wine vinegar, balsamic vinegar or cider vinegar

sea salt and freshly ground black pepper

5 tbs extra virgin olive oil

crushed garlic to taste (optional)

Here's a recipe for the basic dressing that can be used for almost any salad.

METHOD: Mix the mustard with the lemon juice and vinegar and season with salt and pepper. Stir in the olive oil gradually so that the dressing thickens as you work. It should become creamy in consistency. Stir in the garlic (if using). Allow to stand for up to 30 minutes before using, to allow the flavours to develop.

POPPY SEED DRESSING v

MAKES 1 pint (600 ml)

2 oz (50g) caster sugar or honey

1 tbs mild mustard

4 tbs red wine vinegar

sea salt

3 tbs grated sweet onion

14 fl oz (400ml) extra virgin olive oil

3 tbs poppy seeds

2 tbs fresh lemon juice

METHOD: Combine the sugar or honey, mustard, vinegar, salt to taste and grated onion in a food processor and run the machine for 1 minute. Then pour in the oil in a slow steady stream with the machine running. When all the oil has been incorporated, check the seasoning. Stir in the poppy seeds and lemon juice. Keep refrigerated until ready to use.

GARLIC MUSTARD DRESSING v

MAKES about 14 fl oz (400 ml)

juice of 1/2 lemon

3-4 tbs mild mustard

4 tbs red wine vinegar

sea salt and freshly ground black pepper

6 cloves garlic, crushed

1/2 pint (300ml) extra virgin olive oil

METHOD: Put the lemon juice, mustard and vinegar into the blender and season with salt and pepper. Blend until well mixed, then add the garlic. Start adding the olive oil in a dribble, gradually increasing to a slow steady stream. When all the oil has been incorporated check the seasoning. Store in an airtight container in the fridge.

LEMONY CAPER VINAIGRETTE v

MAKES about ½ pint (300 ml)

¼ pint (150ml) extra virgin olive oil

4fl oz (125ml) fresh lemon juice

1 tbs capers, chopped

1-2 tbs mild mustard (optional)

snipped fresh chives (optional)

finely chopped shallots (optional)

sea salt and freshly ground black pepper

METHOD: Combine all the ingredients in a screw-top jar and shake until well blended.

THOUSAND ISLAND DRESSING

MAKES about ½ pint (300 ml)

½ pint (300ml) bottled or home-made mayonnaise (see page 86)

4 tbs tomato ketchup

2 tbs finely chopped parsley (optional)

2 tbs finely chopped dill-pickled cucumber (optional)

2 tbs fresh lemon juice

METHOD: Mix all the ingredients together and keep refrigerated until ready to use.

YOGURT DRESSING

FOR 4–6

6 tbs plain yogurt

2 tbs fresh lemon juice

1 tbs grated mild onion

1 tbs celery seed

crushed garlic to taste

finely chopped green or red pepper (optional)

sea salt and freshly ground black pepper

METHOD: Mix all the ingredients together and season to taste.

KEEPING SALAD FRESH

Cut or torn salad leaves, washed and dried in a salad spinner, will keep crisp longer if they are stored in an airtight bag in the refrigerator.

SAUCES AND DIPS

A GOOD SAUCE WILL ENHANCE THE DELICATE FLAVOURS OF MEATLESS DISHES, AND ADDS ELEGANCE AND INTEREST TO HOME-COOKED MEALS. THE RECIPES IN THIS SECTION ARE JUST A SMALL SAMPLE OF THE ENORMOUS WORLDWIDE REPERTOIRE OF SAUCES FOR PASTA, MAIN COURSES, PASTRY DISHES AND VEGETABLES. THICKER SAUCES ARE SERVED AS DIPS FOR RAW VEGETABLES, FRUIT, BREAD AND TORTILLA CHIPS.

MEATLESS BOLOGNESE SAUCE v

FOR 4

1 large onion, sliced

2-3 large cloves garlic, sliced finely

2 tbs olive oil

4oz (125g) mushrooms, sliced

8oz (250g) vegetarian mince

2 x 14oz (400g) cans chopped tomatoes, with juice

1 tbs each chopped fresh parsley and chives

1/4-1/2 tsp cayenne pepper (optional)

sea salt and freshly ground black pepper

This famous sauce is easy and always popular. You can flavour it as you like by adding extra herbs, garlic or spices to suit the family's tastes. It freezes well and is a useful standby to have on hand.

METHOD: Cook the onion and garlic in the oil over a gentle heat, covered with a lid, for 10 minutes or until quite soft. Stir occasionally. Stir in the mushrooms and vegetarian mince and cook, stirring, for 5 minutes. Then add the tomatoes and herbs and simmer for 5–6 minutes or until well amalgamated. Season to taste with cayenne, salt and black pepper.

BÉCHAMEL SAUCE

MAKES ³/₄ pint (450 ml)

2 oz (50 g) butter or margarine

3 tbs plain flour

³/₄ pint (450 ml) skimmed or soya milk, warmed

pinch of grated nutmeg

sea salt and freshly ground pepper

This classic sauce is an essential part of many favourite dishes, such as lasagne.

METHOD: Melt the butter in a small, heavy-bottomed saucepan. Gradually stir in the flour, using a wooden spoon. Add the warm milk slowly, stirring all the time until the sauce thickens. Season to taste with nutmeg, salt and pepper and simmer over a very low heat for 5–6 minutes.

For ½ pint (300 ml) béchamel, use 1½ oz (40 g) butter or margarine, 2 tbs plain flour and ½ pint (300 ml) milk.

CHEESE AND PARSLEY SAUCE

MAKES ³/₄ pint (450 ml)

1½ oz (40 g) margarine

2 tbs plain flour

1 tbs mild mustard

¼ pint (150 ml) skimmed or soya milk

2 oz (50 g) Cheddar cheese, grated

medium bunch of parsley, chopped finely

¼ pint (150 ml) crème fraîche or single cream (or more milk)

freshly ground black pepper

This popular sauce goes wonderfully well with the cottage crunch casserole on page 40. Its flavours also complement the meatless loaf (page 36).

METHOD: Melt the margarine in a heavy-bottomed saucepan and stir in the flour. When well mixed, stir in the mustard. Slowly add the milk, stirring all the time so that the sauce becomes smooth and thick. Add the grated cheese and the parsley and cook gently for 5 minutes. Add the cream or extra milk, stir until completely smooth, and season to taste with black pepper.

MAYONNAISE

MAKES ½ pint (300 ml)

1 free-range egg

1 tsp Dijon mustard

½ pint (300 ml) olive or sunflower oil

sea salt and freshly ground black pepper

fresh lemon juice to taste

The homemade version of this most popular of sauces is far superior to any bought one. Resist any temptation to add the oil faster than the recipe describes: it will not emulsify (thicken) well if you do.

METHOD: Break the egg into the bowl of the blender and add the mustard. Blend until well mixed, then start to add the oil drop by drop, with the machine running. After a while increase to a thin stream; as the mayonnaise thickens you can increase the flow of oil even more. When all the oil has been added, continue to blend for another minute to thicken up the mayonnaise. Season to taste with salt, pepper and lemon juice.

RICH TOMATO SAUCE ▾

FOR 6

3½ lb (1.5 kg) ripe tomatoes, skinned (see page 13), or 2 x 1½ lb (700 g) cans tomatoes, drained

2 tbs olive oil

1 large onion, chopped

2 tbs chopped garlic

6 oz (175 g) tomato purée

1 tbs chopped fresh oregano or tarragon

1 tbs each chopped fresh basil and thyme

sea salt and freshly ground pepper

This goes really well with pasta, as well as with the beanburgers on page 46 and toad in the hole (see page 33).

METHOD: Cut fresh or canned tomatoes into small cubes. Heat the olive oil and sauté the onion and garlic, stirring, for 1 minute. Add the chopped tomatoes and the tomato purée, then the herbs. Stir well and bring to a simmer. Cook over a very low heat, covered, for 20–25 minutes. Season to taste.

SWEET AND SOUR SAUCE v

MAKES ½ pint (300 ml)

¼ pint (150 ml) pineapple juice

3 tbs olive oil

3 tbs light soft brown sugar

1 tbs soy sauce or more to taste

1 inch (2.5 cm) root ginger, peeled and grated finely

2 cloves garlic, crushed

4 tbs fresh lemon juice

1 heaped tbs cornflour

freshly ground black pepper

A classic sauce to go with Chinese egg fried rice (see page 54) or with steamed or grilled vegetables. You can also toss it into stir-fried vegetables just before serving, and it's indispensable at a barbecue!

METHOD: Combine the pineapple juice, oil, sugar, soy sauce, ginger, garlic and 2 tbs of the lemon juice in a saucepan. Heat until the sugar dissolves. Mix the cornflour with the remaining lemon juice, add to the pan and stir until the sauce is smooth and thick. Season with pepper. Simmer very gently for 5 minutes, stirring occasionally.

MIXED WILD MUSHROOM SAUCE

FOR 3–4

12 oz (350g) wild or Chinese mushrooms, e.g. ceps, chanterelles, field mushrooms, shiitake, oyster etc

2 tbs olive oil

sea salt and freshly ground black pepper

2 tbs chopped fresh thyme or 1 tbs dried thyme

½ pint (300 ml) crème fraîche or single cream

2 tbs fresh lemon juice

The exquisite flavours of wild or Chinese mushrooms in this light, creamy sauce makes it the perfect sauce for pasta.

METHOD: Slice the mushrooms into even lengths. Sauté them in the olive oil until the juices run a little; don't let the mushrooms go too soft. Season to taste with salt and pepper. Add the thyme and stir in. Slowly add the crème fraîche or cream and heat through for 3–4 minutes. Add the lemon juice and check the seasoning.

GRAVY ⌄

MAKES 1 pint (600 ml)

1 onion, chopped small

1½ oz (40g) margarine

4oz (125g) mushrooms, chopped small

3-4 tbs gravy granules

1 pint (600ml) boiling water or stock

1-2 tbs soy sauce or tomato purée

sea salt and freshly ground black pepper

A standby for so many meals, this gravy is wonderful with the meatless loaf (page 36), with vegetarian sausages and, of course, dumplings (see page 14).

METHOD: Soften the onion in the margarine for 4–5 minutes over a low heat, covered with a lid. Add the mushrooms and cook until the juices run. Add the gravy granules to the boiling water and stir until thick. Pour on to the vegetables and stir until well amalgamated. Season to taste with soy sauce or tomato purée, and add salt and pepper if necessary.

GUACAMOLE ⌄

FOR 4–6

2 tomatoes, skinned (see page 13) and chopped

juice of 2 large lemons

1 small fresh red chilli, sliced very finely, or 1 x 4oz (125g) can mild green chillies, chopped finely

2 cloves garlic, sliced finely (optional)

4 spring onions, sliced finely (optional)

2 large avocados, mashed

sea salt and freshly ground black pepper

There are endless versions of this famous Mexican avocado dip: here is mine! Serve with tortilla chips, pitta bread, or raw mushrooms, celery, carrots and other crudités of your choice.

METHOD: Combine all the ingredients except the avocado in the food processor and work until very smooth. Stir in the avocado with a fork and season to taste. Put into a decorative bowl.

REFRIED BEAN DIP

FOR 4–6

8oz (250g) canned refried beans

2-3 tbs taco sauce

4oz (125g) Cheddar cheese, grated

4-5 spring onions, sliced finely

1-2 tsp chilli relish

8fl oz (250ml) crème fraîche or soured cream

sea salt

The satisfying flavours and textures of this dip, inspired by Mexican cookery, make it a firm favourite at parties. Taco sauces are widely available in supermarkets and make a useful standby on the larder shelf.
Serve the dip along-side tortilla chips with drinks before a meal, at any time of the year.

METHOD: Heat the refried beans gently, mashing them with the taco sauce. Stir in the cheese until it melts, then add the spring onions and chilli relish to taste. Stir in the crème fraîche or soured cream and heat through. Season with salt, and serve warm or cold.

SPICY CHILLI DIP ▼

FOR 4

6oz (175g) canned tomatoes

6oz (175g) canned kidney beans

1 tbs tomato purée

dash of soy sauce

2 large cloves garlic, crushed

½ red pepper, deseeded and chopped

3 spring onions, sliced

1 fresh red chilli, sliced

sea salt and freshly ground black pepper

chopped fresh coriander to garnish

If you like the heat of chilli, this dip is for you – and it's quite substantial, too, being made with beans. Lovely with corn chips, pitta bread, raw mushrooms and a selection of crudités.

METHOD: Put all the prepared ingredients into the blender and blend until smooth. Season to taste, and serve garnished with chopped coriander.

CHILLI HEAT

If using fresh chillies, remove the seeds and veins first if you want to control the heat.

DESSERTS AND CAKES

VERY FEW PEOPLE CAN RESIST A REALLY DELICIOUS DESSERT OR SLICE OF CAKE, AND JUDICIOUS AMOUNTS OF SOMETHING SWEET AT REGULAR INTERVALS ARE NOT SUCH A BAD THING FOR GENERAL HEALTH. FRUIT DESSERTS ARE WELL-LOVED, ESPECIALLY PIES AND SPONGE PUDDINGS. CLASSIC CAKES ARE ALSO ONE OF THE PLEASURES OF HOME COOKING AND FAMILY LIFE.

PEACH OR PLUM COBBLER

FOR 6

2 lb (1 kg) ripe peaches, skinned, or plums, stones removed

1-2 tbs sugar

1 tsp grated lemon rind

1 tbs fresh lemon juice

For the cobbler topping:

6 oz (175 g) plain flour

pinch of salt

1 oz (25 g) caster sugar

1 tsp baking powder

½ oz (40 g) margarine

1 free-range egg, beaten

2 tbs skimmed milk or single cream

A fruit cobbler epitomizes the best of home cooking. You can use other fruits besides peaches or plums – apples, pears, gooseberries and so on. Delicious served with whipped cream or ice cream. It is a great American classic pudding.

METHOD: Slice the stoned fruit and put into a baking dish with sugar to taste and the lemon rind and juice.

To make the topping, sift the dry ingredients into a bowl and rub in the margarine until it resembles fine breadcrumbs. Fold in the beaten egg and then the milk or cream to bind to a light dough. Knead for a few moments. Divide the dough into 8 portions and shape each into a flat patty. Place them over the top of the fruit. Bake at 200°C/ 400°F/gas 6 for 25–30 minutes or until the cobbler topping is golden brown. Serve warm.

SPONGE PUDDING WITH APRICOTS AND ALMONDS

FOR 3–4

12 oz (350g) ripe apricots, halved and stoned

For the sponge topping:

2 oz (50g) self-raising flour

2 oz (50g) margarine

2 oz (50g) soft brown sugar

1 size-1 free-range egg

½ tsp vanilla essence

milk if needed

2 oz (50g) flaked almonds, toasted and roughly chopped

One of the simplest recipes ever, this is a family favourite at any time of year. If fresh apricots are unavailable use canned apricot halves or dried soaked apricots.

METHOD: To make the sponge topping, sift the flour into a bowl and add the margarine, sugar, egg and vanilla essence. Beat together until light and creamy. If the mixture seems a little dry, add a small amount of milk. Stir in the almonds.

Arrange the apricots in a 1 pint (600 ml) baking dish and cover with the sponge topping. Bake at 170°C/325°F/gas 3 for 30–35 minutes or until the topping is well risen and golden brown. Serve hot, with cream or custard.

APPLE PIE

FOR 4–6

12 oz (350g) sweetcrust pastry (see page 103)

2 oz (50g) ground almonds

1½ lb (750g) cooking apples, peeled and cored

2-3 oz (50-75g) caster sugar

3 cloves

1 oz (25g) margarine

beaten free-range egg to glaze

The best apple pies in the world are made with Bramleys, if you can get hold of them.

METHOD: Butter a 9–10 inch (22.5–25 cm) flan dish or pie tin. Roll out half of the pastry dough and line the dish. Sprinkle with the ground almonds – they stop the pastry going soggy. Slice the apples very thinly and arrange in the pastry case, sprinkling with sugar to taste. Tuck the cloves into the fruit and dot with the margarine.

Moisten the edge of the pastry case. Roll out the rest of the pastry dough and lay over the top. Press the edges together with a fork to seal them. Trim. Make a few slits in the pastry lid and brush the top with beaten egg. Bake at 220°C/425°F/gas 7 for 30–35 minutes or until the pastry is lightly browned. Serve hot or cold.

APPLE SPONGE PUDDING

FOR 4–6

4 oz (125 g) caster sugar

1 size-1 free-range egg

2 oz (50 g) margarine

5 tbs skimmed or soya milk

3 oz (75 g) plain flour

1½ tsp baking powder

½ tsp ground cloves

12 oz (350 g) cooking apples

lemon juice

Here, tender sugar-glazed apples are baked on a sweet sponge base – an ideal pudding for chilly, damp days. Serve with whipped cream or pouring cream.

METHOD: Reserve ½ oz (15 g) of the sugar; put the remaining sugar in a bowl with the egg and whisk until thick and creamy. Heat the margarine and milk in a saucepan and bring to the boil. Pour into the egg and sugar mixture, whisking. Sift together the flour, baking powder and optional cloves and fold into the egg mixture, making sure there are no lumps of flour. Pour the mixture into a greased 9 x 6 inch (22.5 x 15 cm) baking tin.

Peel and core the apples and cut into slices. Arrange on top of the sponge mixture, leaving no gaps. Sprinkle with lemon juice and then with the reserved sugar. Bake at 200°C/400°F/gas 6 for about 40 minutes or until well risen and golden brown. Serve hot or leave to cool before serving, cut into slices.

BAKED CHOCOLATE PUDDING WITH FUDGE SAUCE

FOR 6

6oz (175g) margarine

6oz (175g) light soft brown sugar

6oz (175g) plain flour

2oz (50g) wholemeal flour

2oz (50g) cocoa powder

3 tsp baking powder

4 free-range eggs, beaten

1 tsp vanilla essence

For the fudge sauce:

6oz (175g) light soft brown sugar

7fl oz (200ml) single cream

1oz (25g) margarine

Who can resist this chocolate cake served warm, soaked in fudge sauce.

METHOD: Cream the margarine with the sugar until light and fluffy. Sift the flours with the cocoa and baking powder (tip the bran from the sieve into the mixture). Beat the flour mixture into the creamed mixture alternately with the eggs, beating until light. Add the vanilla. Turn into an 8 inch (20 cm) round ovenproof dish and bake at 190°C/375°F/gas 5 for 40–45 minutes or until a sharp knife inserted in the centre comes out clean.

Meanwhile, make the sauce: put the sugar, cream and margarine into a heavy-bottomed saucepan. Bring to the boil, stirring to dissolve the sugar, and then turn the heat down until the mixture is simmering. Cook for about 5 minutes or until it is thick.

Pour the sauce over the hot pudding and leave to stand for up to an hour or so before eating, so that the cake has a chance to soak up the sauce.

BAKING BLIND

Baking blind means baking a pastry case before it is filled. If after the filling is put in, the tart, quiche, flan, etc is to be baked further, then the pastry case is baked blind only until it is part cooked. If no further baking is to be done after the filling is added, the pastry case is baked blind until it is completely cooked.

Roll out the pastry dough on a lightly floured board and line the tin. Press the dough lightly into the corners and edges, and trim the edge. Prick with a fork in several places, then spread a piece of foil smoothly over bottom and sides of the pastry case; the foil should overlap the rim of the tin by 2 inches (5 cm). Fill with baking beans. (You can buy ceramic baking beans, or simply use dried beans – once baked they cannot be cooked.)

Bake at 200°C/400°F/gas 6 for 10-15 minutes or until just set, then remove the beans and foil. Return to the oven (without the foil and beans) and bake for a further 5 minutes to crisp and brown the pastry slightly. The pastry case is now part cooked. To bake completely, return to the oven (without the foil and beans) and bake for a further 15 minutes or until the pastry is firm and golden brown.

BLUEBERRY TART

FOR 6

12 oz (350 g) Austrian shortcrust pastry (see page 103)

6 oz (175 g) granulated sugar

3 tbs cornflour

pinch of salt

½ pint (300 ml) water

2 lb (1 kg) blueberries

2-3 tbs icing sugar

8 fl oz (250 ml) plain Greek yogurt

Here a sweet almond pastry case holds a rich blueberry filling topped with sweetened yogurt. The blueberries aren't cooked, so they keep their shape as well as their vitamins.

METHOD: Roll out the pastry dough and line a 9 inch (22.5 cm) pie tin, pressing in the pastry evenly with your knuckles. Bake blind (see left) at 190°C/375°F/gas 5 for 20 minutes, then uncover and crisp up for a further 5 minutes. Leave to cool.

Mix together the sugar, cornflour, salt and water in a saucepan and heat gently, stirring, until thick and smooth. Simmer gently for 5 minutes. Add half of the blueberries at a time and mix thoroughly. Cool.

Just before serving, pour the blueberry mixture into the cooked pastry case. Sift the icing sugar into the yogurt, stir well and spoon over the top of the tart just before serving.

BAKEWELL TART

FOR 8

12 oz (350 g) sweetcrust pastry (see page 103)

4-5 tbs raspberry jam

8 oz (250 g) margarine

8 oz (250 g) caster sugar

8 oz (250 g) ground almonds

1 oz (25 g) plain flour

4 free-range eggs, beaten

One of the great traditional recipes of England, this tart consistently lives up to its excellent reputation. Serve it warm or at room temperature.

METHOD: Roll out the pastry dough and line a 12 inch (30 cm) loose-bottomed flan tin. Spread the jam evenly over the bottom. Cream the margarine with the sugar until light and fluffy, then beat in the almonds and add the sifted flour. Beat in the eggs until the mixture is light and smooth. Spread in the pastry case.

Bake at 190°C/375°F/gas 5 for 45 minutes. (Cover the top with a piece of foil if it begins to burn.) Cool on a rack.

LEMON SOUFFLÉ TART

FOR 12

8oz (250g) sweetcrust pastry (see page 103)

4 size-1 free-range eggs, separated

8oz (250g) caster sugar

¼ pint (150ml) fresh lemon juice

2oz (50g) margarine

pinch of salt

2 tbs icing sugar

A party piece, this is complicated to make but a stunning finale to a special meal. It is intensely lemony, incredibly light, and needs only a little single cream to go with it.

METHOD: Roll out the pastry dough and line an 11 inch (28 cm) loose-bottomed flan tin. Bake blind (see page 94) at 220°C/425°F/gas 7 for 15 minutes, then uncover and bake for a further 5 minutes. Cool on a rack.

Beat the egg yolks with half of the caster sugar until thick and pale, then stir in the lemon juice. Put into a heavy-bottomed saucepan and heat gently, gradually adding the margarine. Stir constantly, being careful not to overheat to simmering point, until the mixture thickens. Cool, then chill for 1–2 hours.

Whisk the egg whites with the salt until they make soft peaks. Whisk in the remaining caster sugar 1 tbs at a time and continue whisking until the mixture is stiff and glossy.

Fold one-quarter of the egg whites into the lemon mixture, then carefully fold in the rest. Pour into the baked pastry case and bake at 190°C/375°F/gas 5 for 15 minutes or until the filling is puffed and light golden brown. Cool on a wire rack for at least 1 hour. Just before serving sift the icing sugar over the top.

CHOCOLATE MOUSSE

FOR 4–6

4oz (125g) plain chocolate, broken into small pieces

3 size-1 free-range eggs, separated

1½ tbs water

2 tbs sweet liqueur such as Chartreuse, Amaretto or Grand Marnier

8fl oz (250ml) double cream or crème fraîche

3 tbsp caster sugar

whipped cream and grated chocolate to decorate

A divinely rich dessert that shows why chocolate mousse is such a universal favourite!
For the best flavour, use a good-quality dark dessert chocolate.

METHOD: Put the chocolate in a small heatproof bowl and set in a pan of hot water to melt. Alternatively, melt in the microwave. Set aside to cool slightly.

Combine the egg yolks and water in a large heatproof bowl and set over a pan of simmering water. Whisk for a minute or so until the yolks start to thicken, being extremely careful not to let them curdle. Add the liqueur and continue whisking until the mixture is pale, very thick and increased in volume. Remove from the heat.

Add the melted chocolate to the whisked mixture and fold it in gently but thoroughly.

Whip the cream or crème fraîche until it starts to thicken. Add 1 tbs of the sugar and continue whipping until thick. Fold into the chocolate mixture.

In a clean bowl, whisk the egg whites until soft peaks will form. Add the remaining sugar and continue whisking until stiff. Fold the egg whites into the chocolate mixture.

Spoon the mousse into a serving bowl or individual ramekins. Cover and chill. When ready to serve, decorate with whipped cream and grated chocolate.

CRISPY GINGER NUTS ᵥ

MAKES 18

3 oz (75 g) self-raising flour

3 oz (75 g) wholemeal flour

2½ tsp baking powder

½ tsp bicarbonate of soda

1½ tsp ground cinnamon

3 tsp ground ginger

3 oz (75 g) margarine

2 tbs caster sugar

1½ rounded tbs golden syrup, heated gently

2 oz (50 g) crystallized ginger, chopped small

These gingery biscuits have some crystallized ginger in them which gives a touch of softness in contrast to the crisp bite. They freeze perfectly.

METHOD: Sift the dry ingredients into a bowl (tip in the bran left in the sieve). Rub in the margarine until it resembles fine breadcrumbs. Mix in the sugar, then the warmed golden syrup and the crystallized ginger. Knead to a light dough.

Break off small pieces of dough the size of a walnut, shape into balls and put on to a greased baking sheet. Flatten the balls with a fork. Bake at 200°C/400°F/gas 6 for 12 minutes. Cool on the baking sheet for 5 minutes, then lift carefully on to a rack to cool completely.

CHOCOLATE CHIP COOKIES

MAKES 10 large or 15 medium

4 oz (125 g) margarine

2 oz (50 g) caster sugar

4 oz (125 g) light soft brown sugar

1 free-range egg, beaten

1 tsp vanilla essence

8 oz (250 g) plain flour

1 tsp baking powder

½ tsp salt

6 oz (175 g) chocolate chips

4 oz (125 g) pecan nuts, roughly chopped

These ever-popular cookies have the richness of chocolate and the crunch of nuts (pecans have been suggested, although you could also use walnuts or hazelnuts). They freeze extremely well.

METHOD: Cream the margarine with both of the sugars until light and fluffy. Beat in the egg. Add the vanilla. Sift the flour with the baking powder and salt, and sift again into the bowl. Beat well to mix. Fold in the chocolate chips and the nuts.

Drop spoonfuls of the dough on to a well-greased baking sheet, leaving space around each to allow for spreading. Bake at 190°C/375°F/gas 5 for 15 minutes or until lightly browned. Cool on the baking sheet for 5 minutes before lifting carefully on to a rack to cool completely.

ABOVE: (left to right) Chocolate Chip Cookies, Crispy Ginger Nuts, Oat and Raisin Biscuits

OAT AND RAISIN BISCUITS

MAKES 10

2 oz (50 g) margarine

4 oz (125 g) light soft brown sugar

1 free-range egg

1 tsp vanilla essence

2 oz (50 g) plain flour

½ tsp salt

½ tsp baking powder

1 tsp ground cinnamon

6 oz (175 g) porridge oats

4 oz (125 g) raisins

Great family favourites, these are spiced with a hint of cinnamon. They are delicious with a glass of milk or juice or a cup of tea or coffee.

METHOD: Cream the margarine with the sugar until light and fluffy. Beat in the egg. Add the vanilla. Sift the flour with the salt, baking powder and cinnamon, then beat into the egg mixture. Add the oats and raisins and mix thoroughly together.

Drop spoonfuls of dough on to well-greased baking sheets, leaving space around each to allow for spreading. Bake at 180°C/350°F/gas 4 for 15 minutes. Allow to cool on the baking sheet for 5 minutes, then lift carefully on to a rack to cool completely.

LEMON DRIZZLE CAKE

MAKES a 9 x 5 inch (23 x 13 cm) cake

4oz (125g) margarine

5oz (150g) caster sugar

finely grated rind and juice of 3 lemons

2 size-1 free-range eggs, beaten

6oz (175g) plain flour

2 tsp baking powder

4 tbs skimmed milk

2oz (50g) granulated sugar

For the cream cheese frosting:

8oz (250g) low fat soft cheese

8oz (250g) icing sugar

1 tbs fresh lemon juice

Light but very moist, this lemony cake is perfect for special occasions. Top with the cream cheese frosting for a birthday cake.

METHOD: Cream the margarine with the caster sugar, lemon rind and 1½ tbs of the lemon juice until light and fluffy. Beat in the eggs one at a time. Beat in the sifted flour and baking powder, then add the milk. Beat thoroughly until light. Put into a greased 2lb (1kg) loaf tin and bake at 180°C/350°F/gas 4 for 45 minutes.

Towards the end of the baking time, heat the remaining lemon juice with the granulated sugar until the sugar dissolves. Simmer for 3–4 minutes.

Cool the cake, in the tin, on a rack for 5 minutes, then turn out, upside down. Pierce the base of the cake all over with a skewer, being careful not to break through the top surface of the cake. Spoon the lemon syrup carefully over the base of the cake until all of it has been absorbed. Leave to cool completely before turning the cake right way up.

To make the cream cheese frosting, mash the cheese and slowly sift in the icing sugar, beating until fully incorporated. Stir in the lemon juice.

When the cake is cold, cut it in half horizontally and fill with one-third of the cream cheese frosting. Spread the remaining frosting over the top and sides of the cake.

CHOCOLATE VICTORIA SPONGE WITH CHOCOLATE BUTTER ICING

FOR 8

4 oz (125 g) plain flour
2 tsp baking powder
2 tbs cocoa powder
4 oz (125 g) caster sugar
4 oz (125 g) margarine
2 free-range eggs
1 tsp vanilla essence
For the chocolate butter icing:
3 oz (75 g) margarine
12 oz (350 g) icing sugar, sifted
1 tbs cocoa powder
1-2 tbs strong black coffee
1½ oz (40 g) grated chocolate

This light chocolate sponge, filled and iced with chocolate butter icing, never fails to please. It is easy to make too.

METHOD: Sift the flour, baking powder and cocoa into a large bowl. Add the caster sugar. Rub in the margarine until it resembles fine breadcrumbs. Beat in the eggs, beating until the mixture is very light. Add the vanilla and beat again.

Put the mixture into a greased 8 inch (20 cm) round loose-bottomed cake tin. Bake at 170°C/325°F/gas 3 for 30 minutes. Leave to cool in the tin for a couple of minutes, then carefully turn out on to a wire rack to cool completely.

To make the icing, cream the margarine with the sifted icing sugar and cocoa until well blended. Add enough coffee to make a spreadable consistency, then fold in the grated chocolate.

When the cake is cold, cut it in half horizontally and fill with one-third of the chocolate butter icing. Cover the top and sides of the cake with the remaining icing.

THE ELECTRIC MIXER

This is indispensable for making cakes and biscuits, as well as many desserts. It beats air into a mixture in a way that even the strongest of wrists cannot!

EASY SHORTCRUST PASTRY ∨

MAKES 9 oz (275 g)

3 oz (75 g) margarine

large pinch of fine sea salt

6 oz (175 g) plain flour

3 tbs cold water

METHOD: Put all the ingredients into the blender or food processor and blend until amalgamated and crumbly. Knead to a smooth dough on a floured board, then chill for at least 30 minutes before using.

If you don't have a blender or food processor, sift the flour with the salt into a bowl and rub in the margarine, lifting the mixture to incorporate as much air as possible. When the mixture resembles fine breadcrumbs, bind with the water. Knead on a floured board until smooth.

AUSTRIAN SHORTCRUST PASTRY

MAKES 1 lb (500 g)

5 oz (150 g) margarine

5 oz (150 g) plain flour

3 oz (75 g) caster sugar

3 oz (75 g) ground almonds

1 free-range egg yolk

1 tsp grated lemon rind

METHOD: Rub the margarine lightly into the sifted flour until the mixture resembles fine breadcrumbs. Stir in the sugar and ground almonds. Mix in the egg yolk and lemon rind and knead on a lightly floured board until smooth. Chill for 30 minutes. When ready to use, roll out to $\frac{1}{4}$ inch (6 mm) thickness.

SWEETCRUST PASTRY ∨

MAKES 12 oz (350 g)

8 oz (250 g) plain flour

1 tbs caster sugar

4 oz (125 g) margarine

3 tbs cold water

METHOD: Sift the flour into a large bowl and stir in the sugar. Rub in the margarine lightly until the mixture resembles fine breadcrumbs. Bind with the water. Knead lightly on a floured board until smooth. Wrap and chill for at least 30 minutes before rolling out.

PUFF PASTRY ∨

MAKES 1 lb (500 g)

8 oz (250g) plain flour

pinch of salt

8 oz (250g) margarine

¼ pint (150ml) ice cold water

squeeze of fresh lemon juice

METHOD: Sift the flour with the salt into a bowl and rub in a walnut-size piece of margarine. Bind with the water and lemon juice and knead to make a smooth dough. Chill for 15 minutes.

Roll out the dough to an oblong. Place the margarine, in a block, in the centre. Wrap the dough around the margarine like a parcel and turn over. **Roll out to an oblong again, fold in three (the bottom third up and the top third down) and press the side edges to seal them. Give the dough a quarter turn so that these edges are at the top and bottom.** Repeat from ** to **. Wrap in greaseproof paper or a teacloth and chill for 15 minutes. Repeat from ** to ** six more times, chilling between each of these 'turns'. Chill for 10 minutes before rolling out finally for baking. Bake at 220°C/425°F/gas 7.

THE VEGETARIAN PANTRY

BASIC PROCESSED FOODS

- canned tomatoes
- canned sweetcorn
- canned beans: cannellini, butter, red kidney, borlotti, flageolet etc
- canned baked beans
- pasta: wholemeal and plain
- wholemeal bread
- soya products: soya milk, tofu, tempeh, vegetarian mince, vegetarian steak chunks, soy sauce, tamari
- vegetable stock cubes
- vegetarian gravy mix
- Marmite, yeast extract
- curry powder
- tomato purée
- tomato ketchup, pickles, relishes, chutneys, mustards
- mayonnaise
- Oriental sauces: black bean, garlic, yellow bean, etc
- Mexican taco sauces and relishes

FROZEN PRODUCTS

- there is now a wide range of readymade frozen vegetarian meals available from supermarkets, including my own brand. These convenient products are ideal for busy cooks

DAIRY PRODUCTS

- free-range eggs
- vegetarian cheese
- plain yogurt

SPREADS, OILS AND VINEGARS

- polyunsaturated margarine (read the label for hidden animal products)
- tahini
- vegetable pastes
- vinegars: cider, wine, rice, balsamic
- olive oil
- vegetable oils: sunflower, grapeseed, soya, groundnut
- dark sesame oil
- walnut oil
- honey, jams (low sugar and homemade), maple syrup

CEREALS

- barley, buckwheat, cornmeal, millet, oats, wheat
- rice
- wild rice
- unbleached organic flour

DRIED FRUIT

- raisins, sultanas, currants
- apples
- apricots
- glacé cherries
- mixed peel
- peaches
- pears
- prunes

DRIED PULSES

- dried beans: black, black-eye, borlotti, butter, haricot, flageolet, mung, red kidney, soya
- lentils: red, green, brown
- split peas
- chick peas

BASIC PLANT FOODS

- nuts: almonds, brazils, cashews, hazelnuts, peanuts, pecans, pine kernels, pistachios, walnuts
- seeds: pumpkin, sesame, sunflower, poppy
- dried coconut
- capers
- olives
- sun-dried tomatoes
- chillies: dried and in brine

HERBS AND SPICES

- sea salt, peppercorns
- vanilla: pods, extract
- herbal teas
- the complete range: fresh and dried herbs, whole and ground spices, to your taste

FRUIT AND VEGETABLES

- plenty of fresh, organic fruit and vegetables in season

PULSES

Pulses, which include beans, peas and lentils, are very versatile, and they are an excellent source of protein, carbohydrate, vitamins and minerals, as well as being low in fat and high in fibre. The soya bean is the best source of quality protein.

Dried pulses need to be soaked overnight, in plenty of water to cover, before cooking. The exceptions are lentils and split peas: large whole lentils and large split peas need only 2–3 hours soaking, and very small red lentils and small split peas need no soaking at all.

To cook pulses, drain off the soaking water and rinse them, then put into a saucepan and cover with fresh water. (If cooking red kidney beans, bring to the boil, boil for 10 minutes, then drain and put back in the pan with fresh cold water to cover.) Add a bay leaf and a slice or two of onion for extra flavour. Bring to the boil and simmer, covered, for the time given in the chart below. Wait to add salt until 10 minutes before the end of the cooking time – it toughens the skins and hardens them if you add it earlier.

Dried pulses double their weight after being soaked and cooked, so when using them instead of canned pulses in a recipe, use half the weight of the canned pulses given. In other words, for 8 oz (250 g) canned kidney beans, soak and cook 4 oz (125 g) dried kidney beans.

When using canned pulses in a recipe, it's best to add them towards the end of the cooking time so that they don't go mushy. Drain them well and rinse them under running cold water before you use them.

COOKING TIMES FOR PULSES, AFTER SOAKING

Aduki beans	30–60 minutes
Black-eye beans	1½ hours
Borlotti beans	1 hour
Butter beans	1–1½ hours
Cannellini beans	1 hour
Chick peas	1½–2 hours
Flageolets	45 minutes
Haricot beans	1–1½ hours
Lentils, large brown or green	45 minutes
Mung beans	40 minutes
Red kidney beans	1–1½ hours
Soya beans	3–4 hours
Split peas, large	40–50 minutes

COOKING TIMES FOR PULSES WHICH REQUIRE NO PRE-SOAKING

Lentils, small red	20–30 minutes
Split peas, small	45–60 minutes

SOYA PRODUCTS

The soya bean is the seed of the soya bean plant. It has been used as a staple in the Chinese diet for more than 4,000 years. From the soya bean come many soya products that are widely used in a vegetarian diet. These include:

• soya milk, which is made by soaking soya beans in water and then straining. Soya cheese and soya yogurt are made from soya milk.

• tofu, which is a curd made from coagulated soya milk. (Vegans can use tofu in place of yogurt in soups, dips, salad dressings and sauces. 'Silken' tofu, which is widely available, is light and creamy and works very well in all these recipes.)

• tempeh, which is a fermented soya bean paste made by mixing cooked soya beans with a fungus that holds it together.

• miso, which is a fermented condiment made from soya beans, grain (rice or barley), salt and water.

• soya or soy sauce (shoyu), which is made by fermenting soya beans with cracked roasted wheat, salt and water.

• tamari, another soy sauce, similar to shoyu but slightly stronger and made without wheat.

- soya margarine and soya oil, both of which are high in polyunsaturated fats and low in saturated fats.
- soya flour
- TVP, or textured vegetable protein, which is de-fatted soya flour, processed and dried to provide a substance that has a spongy texture, similar to meat. A good source of fibre and high quality protein, TVP is also fortified with vitamin B12.

WHEAT

Wheat protein, which is derived from wheat gluten, can be processed to resemble closely the texture of meat and is widely used as a meat substitute.

COOKING WITH MEAT SUBSTITUTES

Meat substitutes are available as mince and chunks, as well as sausages and burgers. All can be found in supermarkets and health food stores. The joy of using vegetarian mince and chunks is that you can take them straight from the freezer – there's no need to thaw them. Just measure out the amount called for in the recipe and add it as directed. You can use them in curries, for spaghetti or lasagne – any dish where you would expect to find mince or stewing steak. (Readers in Great Britain can also find mince and chunks in chilled form – use them exactly as you would the frozen version.)

To brown vegetarian mince or steak chunks (which brings out their flavour), sauté them lightly in 2 tbs hot oil for each 8 oz (250 g). If you are in a hurry you can use these products without browning them first, although they will be slightly less tasty.

As a general rule, every 1 lb (500 g) mince or chunks needs at least ¾ pint (450 ml) liquid in their sauce since they are usually more absorbent than meat. Neither vegetarian mince nor chunks need much salt, so season judiciously.

VEGETARIAN CHEESE

To make cheese, a substance called rennet is used to coagulate milk, separating it into curds and whey. The curds are treated to make cheese, and the liquid whey finds its way into margarines and many other products. Vegetarian cheese is made with rennets of non-animal origin.

Fig leaves, thistle, melon and safflower have provided the country housewife with plant rennets in the past, but today most vegetarian cheeses are made using rennet produced by a fungus, Mucor miehei, or from a bacteria (Bacillus subtilis). Animal rennet, which contains the enzyme chymosin, is usually obtained from the stomach of newly born calves. Advances in genetic engineering have led to the synthesizing of chymosin, which may soon replace animal rennet.

Vegetarian cheeses are usually clearly labelled. Vegetarian versions of cream cheese and other soft cheeses, Cheddar, Cheshire, double Gloucester, stilton, brie, dolcelatte and other blue cheeses, feta and ricotta can all be found in major supermarkets. Cottage cheese is always vegetarian. Parmesan is normally made with animal rennet, although a vegetarian version is emerging. Mozzarella is not always vegetarian.

Cheese is a good source of protein, as well as calcium, zinc, vitamin B12 and a little iron. New vegetarians should be wary of eating too much cheese as it contains a lot of saturated fat and can lead to high cholesterol levels.

MUSHROOMS

In some parts of the world gathering wild mushrooms is a national pastime, a family outing to harvest the ceps, chanterelles, boletus, parasol and field mushrooms that grow in the woods and fields at certain times of the year. Gathering mushrooms is a wonderful experience, akin to a treasure hunt, and you are well rewarded when you deliver them to the table.

Obviously you have to be careful not to pick the wrong ones, but the poisonous mushrooms are easily identifiable with a good field guide. So take to the woods and fields and enjoy the pleasures of both the hunt and the table.

NUTRITION FOR VEGETARIANS

A good diet is a balanced diet: it is the overall mixture that counts. The important thing is to eat a wide variety of foods to give you the nutrients that the body needs to maintain growth, to repair itself, to provide energy, and to resist infection. At least once a day, everyone should eat a well-balanced meal, which means one that contains sufficient carbohydrate, protein, fat, dietary fibre, water, vitamins and minerals for individual needs. These dietary needs vary according to sex, age, activity levels, physical condition and climate. These guidelines should help ensure that you are getting a good nutritional balance in your diet.

ENERGY AND WATER

Food is the fuel that gives the human body energy, thus enabling it to work. The right amount of food is essential for normal biological processes such as breathing and pumping blood round the body, to perform muscular work and to maintain body temperature. Certain foods provide more energy than others; some provide it quickly while others release it slowly into the system.

Water comprises two-thirds of our body weight, and we cannot survive for more than a few days without water. Many foods contain high levels, but it is also important to drink sufficient water on a daily basis: experts suggest $1\frac{3}{4}$–$3\frac{1}{2}$ pints (1–2 litres) every day.

PROTEIN

Proteins are made up from various combinations of amino acids that are required by our bodies for growth and repair. Both plant proteins and animal proteins contain these amino acids, so it is a fallacy that we can only get protein from an animal source. Excess amounts of protein cannot be stored in the body, so eating more than you need can have no benefit. In fact, it can be harmful – many western meat-eating diets contain far too much protein and this is now thought to cause diseases including certain cancers and osteoporosis, as well as poor kidney function.

A healthy, balanced diet containing a variety of foods will provide all the protein you require.

GOOD SOURCES OF PROTEIN Pulses, soya products (tofu, soya milk, etc), nuts, seeds, rice, pasta, wheat flour, bread, muesli, oatmeal, cheese, eggs, milk, yogurt, potatoes, peas, cauliflower, broccoli, garlic, sweetcorn.

CARBOHYDRATE

Carbohydrate is a major source of energy in the diet, and most of it is provided by plant foods. There are three main types of carbohydrate in food: sugars, starches and cellulose. Cellulose is the indigestible part of plant foods and is the main constituent of dietary fibre. This stimulates the digestive system, helps prevent constipation and reduces the risk of colon cancer and disease.

GOOD SOURCES OF CARBOHYDRATE Pulses, rice, pasta, buckwheat groats, bulgar wheat, oatmeal, bread, nuts, potatoes, root vegetables, peas, sweetcorn, onions, garlic, dried apricots, bananas, mangoes.

GOOD SOURCES OF DIETARY FIBRE Pulses, nuts, wholemeal bread, wholemeal pasta, wheat bran, oats and other whole grains, most vegetables, raspberries, blackberries, redcurrants, dates, figs, prunes, dried apricots.

FAT AND CHOLESTEROL

Fat provides energy in a more concentrated form than carbohydrate and converts very easily into body fat. Although a certain amount of fat is necessary to provide warmth and essential nutrients and to protect the internal organs, the average western diet contains too much. Fats from animal sources contain a high proportion of saturated fatty acids, which raise blood cholesterol levels and increase the risk of heart disease.

Cholesterol is unique to animals and humans. It is made mainly in the liver and is present in all of the body's tissues. We need cholesterol but we do not necessarily need it in the diet: for some people an excess can cause health problems. This is why people on a diet containing no animal products are thought to be less at risk from heart disease.

SOURCES OF FAT Cheese, cream, yogurt, whole milk, butter, margarine, egg yolk, nuts, seeds, avocados, olives, vegetable oils, oats.

VITAMINS

Small amounts of vitamins are essential for the regulation of all bodily processes. With the exception of vitamin D, the body cannot make its own vitamins, and some cannot be stored. Vitamins must therefore be obtained from food on a daily basis. A vegetarian diet can provide all the necessary vitamins.

VITAMIN A

Required for healthy skin and mucus membranes, and for night vision. Thought to help prevent the development of cancer.

GOOD SOURCES OF VITAMIN A Butter, margarine, milk, cheese, yogurt, cream, sweet potatoes, butternut squash, carrots, red peppers, chillies, leeks, lettuce, broccoli, Swiss chard, spinach, tomatoes, watercress, basil, coriander, parsley, apricots, canteloupe melons, mangoes.

B VITAMINS

A group of eight actual vitamins and several vitamin-like compounds. The main ones include:
Thiamin (B1): Releases energy from carbohydrate, alcohol and fat.
Riboflavin (B2): Releases energy from protein, fat and carbohydrate.
Niacin (B3): Involved in the oxidative release of energy from food; protects the skin and helps improve circulation.
Vitamin B6: Essential for protein metabolism, and for the formation of haemoglobin.
Vitamin B12: Helps protect nerves and is involved in the formation of red blood cells.
Folate: Involved in the formation of new cells and therefore essential for the normal growth and development of the foetus.

GOOD SOURCES OF B VITAMINS Eggs, cheese, milk, pulses, wholemeal bread, brown rice, fortified breakfast cereals, nuts, seeds, yeast extract, avocados, cauliflower, cabbage, peas, potatoes, mushrooms, green leafy vegetables, dates, figs, currants, dried apricots, clementines, canteloupe melon.

VITAMIN C

Essential for the formation of bones, teeth and tissues. Speeds the healing of wounds, helps maintain elasticity of the skin, aids the absorption of iron and improves resistance to infection. May help prevent the occurrence and development of cancer.

GOOD SOURCES OF VITAMIN C Broccoli, Brussels sprouts, cauliflower, cabbage, mangetout, green leafy vegetables, red peppers, chillies, watercress, parsley, blackcurrants, strawberries, kiwi fruit, guavas, citrus fruit.

NOTE: With the exception of niacin (B3), these vitamins are easily destroyed by heat. Vitamin C is easily destroyed by exposure to air, and all are unstable in alkaline conditions and are water-soluble. So to maximize the intake of these vitamins, food sources should be prepared, cooked and served quickly. Steaming vegetables minimizes vitamin loss.

VITAMIN D

Needed for the absorption of calcium and the regulation of calcium levels in the blood. Sunlight activates the metabolism of vitamin D in the body.

GOOD SOURCES OF VITAMIN D Butter, margarine, cheese, cream, yogurt, milk, eggs, sunlight.

VITAMIN E

An anti-oxidant that protects the cells from attack by reactive forms of oxygen and free radicals. Involved in red blood cell formation.

GOOD SOURCES OF VITAMIN E Vegetable oils, nuts and nut oils, seeds, egg, margarine, hard cheeses, chickpeas, soya beans and soya products, wheat germ, oatmeal, avocados, olives, carrots, parsnips, red peppers, green leafy vegetables, sweet potatoes, tomatoes, sweetcorn, watercress.

VITAMIN K

Needed for effective blood clotting. A deficiency is rare due to bacterial synthesis within the body. Vitamin K is found in most vegetables.

MINERALS

Minerals perform a variety of important functions in the human body. A balanced intake is important for long-term good health. Excess of any mineral can be as dangerous as too little.

CALCIUM

Calcium is the most abundant mineral in the body, and is needed for building strong bones and teeth, for muscle contraction and blood clotting. Healthy bones are not only reliant on a good calcium intake but on regular exercise and vitamin D, which aids calcium absorption.

It should also be noted, however, that too much calcium can also be harmful as the excess is deposited in internal organs such as kidneys. This can cause serious problems and even be fatal.

Dairy foods have traditionally been thought of as the principal source of calcium, but have you ever stopped to think where the cow gets its calcium from – certainly not from dairy products!

GOOD SOURCES OF CALCIUM Milk, cheese, yogurt, sesame seeds, tofu, bread, nuts, pulses, okra, broccoli, watercress, onions, green leafy vegetables, sea vegetables, dried fruit such as raisins, apricots, pears and peaches, rhubarb, lemons, oranges, hard water.

MAGNESIUM

Needed for strong bones, and for the functioning of some of the enzymes involved in energy utilization.

GOOD SOURCES OF MAGNESIUM Cream, yogurt, cheese, eggs, bread, papadums, wheat bran, bulgar wheat, oatmeal, soya flour, wholemeal flour, brown rice, wholemeal pasta, nuts, seeds, pulses, green leafy vegetables, sea vegetables, dried fruit such as apricots, pears and peaches.

IRON

Essential component of haemoglobin, the red pigment in blood which transports oxygen though the body. Iron also assists in the production of red blood corpuscles, the metabolism of B vitamins and the functioning of several enzymes. Iron deficiency, which causes anaemia, is the most prevalent nutritional problem worldwide. It has been shown that vegetarians are no more likely to suffer from it than non-vegetarians. A good intake of vitamin C enhances absorption of iron.

GOOD SOURCES OF IRON Eggs, pulses, wholemeal bread, wheat bran, papadums, cashew nuts, pine nuts, pumpkin seeds, cumin seeds, sesame seeds, green leafy vegetables, watercress, sea vegetables, basil, mint, parsley, blackcurrants, dried fruits such as raisins, prunes, figs and peaches, cocoa.

ZINC

Present in every part of the body and vital for the healthy working of many of its functions, including a major role in enzyme reactions, the immune system and resistance to infection. It plays a crucial role in growth and cell division, in insulin activity and liver function. Men need more zinc than women because semen contains 100 times more zinc than is found in the blood, and so the more sexually active a man is, the more zinc he will require.

GOOD SOURCES OF ZINC Cheese, egg yolk, pulses, wholemeal bread, wheat bran, soya flour, yeast, nuts, pumpkin seeds, sesame seeds, tahini paste, green vegetables, garlic.

POTASSIUM

Important in maintaining the body's correct balance of fluids, required for nerve and muscle function, and the metabolism of sugar and protein.

GOOD SOURCES OF POTASSIUM Yogurt, pulses, soya flour, nuts, seeds, green vegetables, potatoes, beetroot, chillies, garlic, sea vegetables, rhubarb, bananas, dates, dried apricots, prunes.

INDEX

Page numbers in *italic* refer to the illustrations

Linda's *winter* Kitchen